Behind the Bamboo Hedge

The Impact of Homeland Politics in the Parisian Vietnamese Community

Gisèle L. Bousquet

Ann Arbor
THE UNIVERSITY OF MICHIGAN PRESS

1994   1993   1992   1991   4   3   2   1

Library of Congress Cataloging-in-Publication Data

Bousquet, Gisele L. (Gisele Luce), 1952–
    Behind the bamboo hedge : the impact of homeland politics in the
Parisian Vietnamese community / Gisele L. Bousquet.
        p.   cm.
    Includes bibliographical references and index.
    ISBN 0-472-10174-9 (alk. paper)
    1. Vietnamese — France — Paris — Political activity.   2. Refugees,
Political — France — Paris — Social Conditions.   3. Anti-communist
movements — France — Paris.   4. Paris (France) — Ethnic relations.
5. Vietnam — Politics and government — 20th century — Influence.
I. Title.
DC718.V53B68   1991
944′.360049592 — dc20   90-48472
                                                                    CIP

Distributed in the United Kingdom and Europe by
Manchester University Press, Oxford Road,
Manchester M13 9PL, UK

To Jacqueline Bousquet and Elizabeth Colson

Acknowledgments

This book could not have been completed without the time, energy, and support of others. First, I want to express my deepest appreciation to Elizabeth Colson, who, throughout my graduate training, has been a shining example of all that an anthropologist could and ought to be. As a critic and as a role model, her support has been invaluable.

I wish to thank George De Vos for both intellectual and moral support, James Anderson for his meticulous and thorough review of my work, Frederick Wakeman and Paul Rabinow for their valuable critical comments on the manuscript, and James Freeman for his intellectual and editorial guidance of the final revision of the book.

I am grateful to Pierre Brocheux, whose knowledge of Vietnam and the Parisian Vietnamese community was crucial for the conduct of my research, to François Raveau for his hospitality at Centre Richet pour l'Etude sur le Dysfonction de l'Adapation (CREDA), and to John Ogbu and Jack Potter for their support and encouragement.

I would also like to thank my colleagues and friends at the University of California, Berkeley, including: Suzanne Bowler, Daniel Maltz, and Ann Wooldrige for editing endless revisions of the manuscript. Warm thanks to Helene Knox for her editorial work and moral support.

Translations from French and Vietnamese are my own. I would like to thank Catherine Benoît for editing the French texts. I am also grateful to Chung Hoang Chuong for his assistance with the Vietnamese texts.

I am also grateful to Michelle and Martine Laviec for their warm hospitality and moral support in Paris, and to my mother and my brothers and sisters for their wisdom and understanding.

Finally, my appreciation goes to the Vietnamese people, for allowing me to study their community behind the bamboo hedge.

This research was supported by the Institute of International Studies at the University of California, Berkeley, through its apprenticeship program, and by the John L. Simpson Fellowship.

Contents

Chapter 1

Introduction

In a windowless room in San Jose, 100 South Vietnamese
war veterans plotted strategies yesterday to liberate their former nation. (S. Magagnini, *San Francisco Chronicle*, October
7, 1985:6)

To the general public, political activity among refugee groups is not
a new issue. In fact, the media periodically report on immigrant political activities. Yet social scientists have paid relatively little attention to politics among immigrants (Portes and Mozo 1985). Today,
Europe and the United States have large immigrant populations of
political refugees and expatriates: Vietnamese, Armenians from
Turkey, Palestinians, Afghans, and Cubans, among others. These
people continue to organize their communities around homeland
political issues. The majority of them involved in political organizations have had some higher education and have achieved some
degree of socioeconomic integration into their adoptive countries.
After some years in the host country, both the immigrants and the
refugees often give up their status of "resident" to become citizens.
Changing their legal status, however, does not affect their political
allegiance to their homeland. The Cuban-Americans who have
gained political power in Miami are advancing, along with domestic issues, their own political agenda regarding American policies
toward Cuba. The Armenian-Americans published a pledge in the
New York Times (September 22, 1989) to the Soviet Foreign Minister touring the United States:

An appeal to Soviet Foreign Minister Eduard Shevardnadze
. . . Every day an Armenian is killed in Azerbaijan SSR

and Nagorno-Karabagh . . . The Soviet Government must: . . . reverse the Stalinist decisions of 1923 and 1929 to separate Nagorno-Karabagh from Armenia and recognize and respect the universal principle of self-determination for the Armenians of Nagorno-Karabagh.

This advertisement was sponsored by a number of Armenian organizations in the United States and Canada; among them were the Armenian Revolutionary Federation, the Armenian Relief Society, and the Social Democratic Hunchakian Party.

These immigrants and refugees have thus formed international political organizations through which they indirectly participate in governmental decision making in the homeland whenever possible. These international political networks, linking together refugees and immigrants who have resettled outside the home country, represent a vital political force within it as well as in the international political arena. Such overseas political organizations not only give financial support to homeland political parties, but also use their influence in the host country. A recent article on the former Chinese officials who went into exile after the Tiananmen Square massacre in China states:

The federation's leaders asserted that they could exert effective pressure on China's Government even though they are outside of the country. They say they expect to obtain funds from Chinese living in Hong Kong, Singapore, the United States and elsewhere. "There are 56 million Chinese living abroad," Mr. Chen said. "We hope to unite them." (Steven Greenhouse, *New York Times*, September 25, 1989)

Homeland politics is an attribute of both immigrant and refugee groups, although it has been more evident among political refugees. Refugees and immigrants are two distinct sociological categories. They are differentiated by the motivation and decision making of a particular group to uproot itself and resettle elsewhere. Mangalam (1968:8) defines migration as

a relatively permanent moving away of a collectivity, called migrants, from one geographical location to another, preceded by decision making on the part of the migrants on the basis of a hierarchical ordered set of values or valued ends and resulting in changes in the interactional system of migrants.

The pull factor thus plays an essential role in the migrants' decision process for leaving their homeland. On the other hand, the push factor characterizes the exodus of refugees from their country of origin.

The refugees are indeed considered a distinct class of immigrants due to their hasty compulsory departure from their homelands. Kunz (1973:130) suggests

> it is the reluctance to uproot oneself, and the absence of positive original motivations to settle elsewhere, which characterize all refugee decisions and distinguish the refugee from the voluntary migrants.

These two sociological categories are not mutually exclusive, since they are both related to world politics. Through international consensus, the United Nations definition of a refugee is "an individual who owing to well-founded fear of being persecuted . . . is outside the country of his nationality and unable to return to it" (Plender 1972:215). While the refugees have to prove to immigration officials that they have been persecuted in their homeland, each nation reserves the right to grant asylum. Most nations regard themselves as being under a moral obligation to extend their protection to those suffering from persecution. But there is no universal consensus on what constitutes "persecution," so each nation defines it according to its own national and international policies. Article 129 of the constitution of the Soviet Union states:

> The USSR affords the right of asylum to foreign citizens persecuted for defending the interests of the working people, or for scientific activities, or struggling for national liberation. (Plender 1972:228)

The United States, on the other hand, has given the right of asylum to people coming from communist countries, such as, among others, the Vietnamese, Cubans, Afghans, and Jews from the Soviet Union. That same right was denied to Haitians and El Salvadorans, who are considered migrants.

In this book, the distinction between immigrants and refugees is based on these two sociological and political definitions, and on the representation Vietnamese make of themselves. Among Vietnamese in France, the term *immigrants* refers to those Vietnamese who settled in France before the 1975 reunification of Vietnam. The term *refugees* refers to the post-1975 Vietnamese who fled Vietnam after the collapse of the South Vietnamese government under assault from communist troops.

Homeland politics among immigrants and refugees entails political divisions within the overseas communities. These divisions are based on the groups' alliances with different homeland political parties or ideologies. Political organizations in overseas communities do not in themselves constitute political parties, but rather are factional groups. These political groups compete with each other for membership and community financial support. Furthermore, they ally themselves with host country political parties to advance their own political agenda, and they lobby to influence their host country's policy toward their homeland. Although these organizations exert their political power from a distance, their impact on international politics cannot be ignored.

From the late 1950s, anthropologists (Benedict 1957; Boissevain 1966; Nicholas 1965; Siegel and Beals 1960) who focused their studies on small-scale societies suggested that, as conflict groups, factions are noncorporate political groups whose members are recruited by a leader. In the Vietnamese overseas community in France, however, political conflicts emerged from issue-related rather than leader-related conflicts. I suggest that factional political conflict among Vietnamese immigrants, for instance, cannot be understood at the community level, but rather has to be seen as part of a multidimensional set of relations that involve diplomatic relations and general ties between Vietnam, France and other Western countries, and the worldwide Vietnamese overseas communities.

The arrival of thousands of Vietnamese refugees in the United States, France, Australia, and Canada has been the subject of many studies that, however, mainly address issues related to the refugees' socioeconomic integration into the host country. In the United States, a large number of studies have focused on the refugees' adaptation and problems associated with resettlement during the first five post-flight years (Kelly 1977; Liu 1979; Montero 1979; Starr and Roberts 1982; Stein 1979; Strand 1984). All of these studies date from the period following the fall of Saigon.

In France, similar research was carried out first in 1954, when a large number of Vietnamese expatriates arrived there after the Geneva agreement (Simon 1981; Simon-Barouh 1982). Then, after 1975 and the fall of Saigon, a new influx of Vietnamese immigrants prompted new studies (Bonvin and Pinchaud 1981; Mignot 1984; Thuan Cao Huy 1984; Simon 1981).

In the United States and France, these studies addressed the individual's immediate occupational, economic, social, cultural, and mental adaptation to the host country (Carkroff 1979; Liu 1979; Montero 1979; Nguyen 1982; Nicassio 1985; Stein 1979; Strand and Jones 1985). By the mid-1980s, Vietnamese refugees had recovered from the initial shock of resettlement, and had formed stable overseas communities. The present study examines this community in France at its second stage of adaptation and focuses on the group rather than the individual.

Vietnamese immigrants in France have long been involved in political activities related to homeland issues. The Parisian Vietnamese community is both one of the oldest overseas Vietnamese communities, and a highly politicized one; politics, characterized by factionalism, plays an essential role in the community. Since 1975, the Vietnamese community has been polarized into two major political factions: pro-Hanoi and anticommunist (Girardet 1980). The older cohorts of immigrants were dominated by leftist ideologies. The arrival of a large number of political refugees in France in 1975, after the fall of the Saigon government, changed the political makeup of the community. Refugee anticommunist organizations began to emerge as a political force opposing the established leftist Vietnamese community. The pro-Hanoi and anticommunist factions now compete with each other to gain the support of newly arrived refugees.

Although this book deals essentially with homeland politics in the Parisian Vietnamese community, the fervent political conflict dividing the French Vietnamese community also exists in the American Vietnamese community.

In France, the pro-Hanoi faction dominates the political arena of the Vietnamese community, whereas in the United States the anticommunist organizations are the most visible and powerful faction. As in the French Vietnamese political organizations, the members and leaders of such organizations in the United States are educated people, including intellectuals, professionals, and former political activists and leaders in Vietnam.

The anticommunist organizations, having as leaders former South Vietnamese leaders, speak openly and freely against Hanoi and Vietnamese communism. It would be misleading, however, to believe that these organizations will fade away as soon as these leaders withdraw from the political scene. The torch has indeed been passed to a younger generation. I have met a number of Vietnamese youths, mostly university students, a generation too young to have witnessed the war, who carry on the same fervent political discourse on Vietnam. These organizations have their headquarters in San Jose and Los Angeles, areas that have the largest populations of Vietnamese in California. The presence and impact of these organizations is visible in the Vietnamese community. The yellow and red flag of the pre-1975 South Vietnamese government in the windows of Vietnamese shops and restaurants in San Jose is a constant reminder of the community's loyalty to these organizations.

The pro-Hanoi faction, known by the Vietnamese in France as the "Union" organization, is viable in the United States, although since the arrival of refugees in 1975, it has kept a low profile in the Vietnamese community. Members were former Vietnamese students who had come to the United States to pursue their studies. In the late 1960s, they participated in the American antiwar movement. According to my informants, they portray themselves as "liberals," whereas the Vietnamese anticommunist leaders label them "communists" or agents of Hanoi infiltrating the Vietnamese community. Because of their well-founded fear of reprisal from the anti-communists, the members of the Union no longer publicly speak or expose their political ideologies. I am purposely choosing not to reveal to the reader further information regarding this organization, because the issue is still too sensitive in the American Vietnamese community.

In France also the anticommunist organizations compete with the pro-Hanoi faction for community support. Anticommunist political activities involve demonstrations, political debate, and open criticism against the government of Hanoi in their own newspapers. In the United States their quest for political power in the community has included using violence against the so-called Vietnamese communists. The use of many forms of intimidation tactics to control the community has been a pattern in the American Vietnamese political arena.

I first became aware of the extent of this repression in the American Vietnamese community while doing fieldwork in San Francisco during the summer of 1982. A few months earlier, Lam, a twenty-seven-year-old Vietnamese man, had been shot to death for engaging in what were referred to as communist political activities. The police investigation was at a standstill. In the community, Vietnamese refugees generally were reluctant to cooperate with the police for fear of retaliation from the anticommunist organizations. During my interviews, I questioned informants with whom I had good rapport about the crime. Many did not want to comment, but those who did surprised me with their answers. For instance, Tuan, a thirty-year-old Vietnamese man, told me that Lam was a communist agent who had been trying to recruit the young for his communist group. His job as a social worker had easily enabled him to infiltrate the community. According to Tuan, "communist written materials, along with a picture of Ho Chi Minh, were found in the apartment he rented in the San Francisco Tenderloin." Tuan felt that Lam's propagandizing should have been stopped, but also that he should not have been killed.

Lam was not the only target of this political violence. In 1984, Henry Hung Tieu and his wife Hai Thai Tieu were both murdered in their home in San Francisco. According to my informants in the pro-Hanoi faction in Paris, Mr. Tieu was the leader of the Union, the American Vietnamese pro-Hanoi faction in San Francisco. In the magazine *Insight*, Richard Martin reports:

Tran Khanh Van, a former South Vietnamese official, was shot and wounded in Orange County's Little Saigon in 1986, not long after publicly stating his support for normalization of relations . . . The novelist Long Vu was beaten and left partially paralyzed last year, also in Little Saigon. Vu had written newspaper and magazine articles criticizing both the former South Vietnamese government and the present government in Hanoi. The editor of a Vietnamese-language paper in Houston, Dam Phong, was killed there in 1983. (*Insight*, September, 1989:18)

On August 19, 1989, Doan Van Toai was shot in Fresno because he was considered a threat to Vietnamese anticommunist organizations. Doan Van Toai, the author with David Chanoff of *The Vietnamese Gulag* (1986) and a number of other books, founded the Institute for Democracy in Vietnam, a Washington lobbying group to support the American-Vietnamese diplomatic relationship.

Intimidation short of murder is also used efficiently by the anticommunist organizations. In the spring of 1989, for example, a group of Vietnamese musicians, called "Din Thin, Bamboo Flutes and Nguyen Xuan Hoach, Lutes and Guitars," was touring American cities. In San Francisco, a large Vietnamese anticommunist demonstration against the performance was staged in front of the auditorium. The demonstrators claimed that the performance was communist propaganda. They had brought cameras and video equipment to intimidate Vietnamese people and thus discourage them from participating in the event.

The intimidation tactics worked, since many Vietnamese who otherwise would have participated in the event stayed away. A Vietnamese teacher told me that he had bought tickets in advance for himself and his family. When he heard about the demonstration, he decided not to go for fear of being accused of being a communist. He was especially concerned about having his picture taken and then published in the local Vietnamese newspaper under the title "Communists' Participation."

Thus, the appearance of political uniformity among Vietnamese Americans reflects the active role of the anticommunist organizations in the community to maintain their power. According to my French Vietnamese informants, these organizations indeed play a major role in leading overseas anticommunist Vietnamese organizations.

The Setting

In this study, I have excluded the Chinese-Vietnamese ethnic group although large numbers of them have left Vietnam and many are settled in Paris. I do so because they are not accepted as "Vietnamese" by the ethnic Vietnamese who are the focus of my study. Unlike the ethnic Vietnamese, Chinese-Vietnamese tend to congregate in ghettolike neighborhoods. Many today live in the thirteenth arrondissement, called the "new Parisian Chinatown." My Vietnamese informants call it the "Cholon," after the Chinese sector of Saigon. The Chinese community's extensive social and economic network includes Chinese from Southeast Asia, Taiwan, mainland China, and Hong Kong. The Vietnamese people differentiate themselves from the Southeast Asian Chinese on the grounds that they do not share the same cultural heritage. Nevertheless, in Paris, the Chinese from Southeast Asia are involved in businesses such as restaurants and Asian grocery stores that serve not just the Asian community generally, but the Vietnamese in particular. The Vietnamese feel at home shopping in the Parisian "Chinese area." Other Indochinese populations, such as the Laotians and the Cambodians, also constitute separate cultural communities and, like the Chinese, do not participate in Vietnamese organizations. They have their own social and political organizations that sometimes align with those of the Vietnamese.

The Vietnamese community in Paris is the oldest and largest one in France, with a population officially estimated at fifty thousand. Vietnamese informants, however, think it may be as large as eighty thousand. Like many other immigrants, the Vietnamese find Paris the most desirable place to live. Paris is considered one of the most cosmopolitan cities in Europe, and one where the immigrants can mingle without being singled out. Other French cities and towns are more traditional and tend to reject newcomers of alien origin. In particular, nonwhite immigrants such as Arabs, Chinese, Vietnamese, and Africans fear the "provincials'" racist attitudes. In Paris, the Vietnamese, unlike the Chinese, do not like to live in a specific area. The community has thus spread to all areas of the city. However, the Vietnamese rely on a close-knit social and kinship network for community life.

pose of this study, I differentiate between two cat-
ants: (1) the long-established pre-1975 commu-
ewly arrived refugees (post-1975). The Viet-
nselves in one or the other of these categories.
'ormants, members of the anticommunist or-
_entify themselves as a "refugee" or an "immigrant" in
_. to make a political statement. Anticommunist leaders con-
sider themselves refugees because they have been prohibited from
returning to Vietnam. The immigrants, on the other hand, do not
reject the Hanoi government.

These two communities contrast sharply in the degree of
their socioeconomic integration into French society. The long-
established immigrant group is composed of: (a) retired workers
who were involved in anticolonial movements and whose children
have obtained higher education; (b) refugees from North Vietnam
after 1954; and (c) former students who have entered the French
economy as professionals (lawyers, doctors, university professors).
The newly arrived Vietnamese include Vietnamese professionals,
who have not always found equivalent work in France, and working class Vietnamese with little education. As I anticipated when
I began interviewing, long-standing immigrants tend to be pro-
Hanoi, while those arriving after 1975 oppose the communist regime in Vietnam and had to flee Vietnam as political refugees.

Insider versus Outsider

Since my research deals with the politics of Vietnamese immigrants, I focused my study on their political organizations.
Most of my informants were educated people who belonged to
Vietnamese political organizations. These organizations proved to
be central not only for political activities but also as nodes for large
social networks.

Scholars who conduct field research on Vietnamese immigrants and refugees face a number of problems related to their
informants' attitudes toward outsiders and toward the topics under
study. Vietnamese immigrants and refugees have close-knit social
organizations and dislike talking to strangers about themselves.
Many warned me that the Vietnamese would not tell me the truth
and would rather lie in order to protect their community. I also en-

countered difficulties in getting data, but I utilized my knowledge of the Vietnamese overseas communities and my personal experiences to establish my own network in the community. Although I am not Vietnamese, my discourse on migration is by now that of an insider.

Although of French origin and culture, I am an expatriate living in the United States. As an immigrant, I have, like the Vietnamese immigrants and refugees, experienced the difficulties of adjusting to a foreign culture. Well before I ever began my research, I was closer to the Vietnamese community than to American society. This common experience of immigration turned out to be my most valuable asset in communicating and relating to the Vietnamese.

I first encountered Vietnamese refugees when I arrived in San Francisco in 1975, seven months after the fall of Saigon. By that time, thousands of Vietnamese refugees were being resettled in San Francisco. During my first year in the United States, my life was not so different from that of the Vietnamese refugees. I was holding two jobs and going to school in order to learn English. Being by myself, I spent a great deal of my free time with other immigrants and refugees from China, Latin America, and Vietnam. Although we came from different cultural and social backgrounds, in the United States we were all "foreigners." Because of my French background, the Vietnamese refugees I met at school were friendly toward me. Many of them had been educated in French schools in Vietnam. I became friendly with a number of them and started to develop a particular interest in Vietnam and in their experiences as refugees. This early encounter with the American Vietnamese community, as well as my own status as an immigrant, facilitated my initial contacts with the French Vietnamese immigrants and refugees.

A few years later, as a student of anthropology, I carried out fieldwork in the Vietnamese community, both among Vietnamese refugees in San Francisco and in refugee camps in Hong Kong (summer, 1983). I also took courses in the Vietnamese language to facilitate my communication with them and my understanding of their culture.

I returned to France in 1984 for a year of fieldwork, after almost ten years living abroad. Although I was frank about my cultural identity, I was perceived by both French and Vietnamese people as an insider of the Vietnamese community. Though I was unable to surrender my identity, my physical appearance became the key factor for my belonging to the Vietnamese culture. With my short height, dark hair, and somewhat slanted eyes, I have indeed the physical appearance of a Eurasian, mixed-blood Vietnamese woman. To many French people I encountered, especially in academia, I was perceived as Eurasian. In one instance, a French anthropologist, whom I do not want to identify, tried to convince me that I had all the physical characteristics of a Eurasian.

In the Vietnamese community, especially among the long-established community, I was also considered Eurasian. In social and political gatherings, my presence was barely noticed. When I was accompanied by a Vietnamese friend, it was not unusual for people to ask me if my friend and I were from the same family. On one occasion, after I had been chatting with a representative of the Vietnamese Consulate in Paris during a Sunday lunch at a Buddhist temple, a couple of Vietnamese people asked me if I was his daughter. On another occasion, I had dinner with one of my informants, a leader of an anticommunist Vietnamese political organization. I had met him a number of times before. Throughout the evening, he gave me convincing arguments about why I belonged to the Vietnamese culture. From his own viewpoint, it was not just my physical traits, but also my way of thinking and being that suggested I was of Vietnamese ancestry.

Being perceived as an insider helps me a great deal in working in the Vietnamese community, but I was also torn over the issue of misrepresentation. On the one hand, I wanted to be honest with my informants about my own cultural background and experience. On the other hand, I did not want to be thought of as someone who was denying her own cultural heritage. After a few months, I decided to no longer try to justify my origin. When asked, I replied that I was of French descent but maybe I had Vietnamese ancestry.

I identify myself, however, as a French expatriate. Over the years, I have maintained my bicultural identity by returning frequently to France to visit my family. Although I live abroad, my understanding of French society remains that of an insider.

My interest in politics is a product of my own cultural background. While still a teenager, I learned how to formulate political opinions, although at the time they were naturally quite immature. I was then a fervent critic of my own society. My strong opposition to French ethnocentrism resulted in my departure from France to meet the "others." Back in France, I was quite at ease when working with the "others," the Vietnamese people.

In the context of French culture, it was not considered odd for me to engage in political discussions with my informants. I was, after all, French. The political diversity in France is reflected in the wide spectrum of political parties. As a topic, politics is commonly discussed in one's encounters with people. Although I enjoy political discussions, I never belonged to any French political party, but carried my interest and curiosity over to Vietnamese politics. Among the Vietnamese, however, this topic embraces other factors, which are further discussed in this chapter.

Doing Fieldwork in an Urban Setting

As a graduate student, I was taught that an anthropologist ought to live in the community that he or she was studying. In my fieldwork situation I was dealing with two issues. The first related to the fact that the Vietnamese people did not live in a specific area in Paris. The second was the nature of my research, which required working with both factional political organizations. While looking for a place to live, on a number of occasions I had contemplated the idea of taking my informants up on their offers to have me live with them and their families. Each time, however, I decided to decline the offer in order to maintain my neutral position toward my informants of both factions. Because I lived alone or with French friends, my informants from either side were able to phone and visit me freely without the knowledge of anyone from the Vietnamese community.

My fieldwork consisted of establishing my own network in each of the political factions, and obtaining data on the activities of the political organizations. At the beginning of the fieldwork, my interviews were sketchy. Although my contacts with informants were comfortable because of my personal background, the informants tended not to disclose information regarding political activities in the community. The more I got to know the community, however, and gathered information on my own, the more credible I became.

I visited many community organizations and businesses, and contacted French organizations and social service groups working with Vietnamese refugees. I participated in social and cultural events sponsored by Vietnamese organizations, and sometimes I was invited to private social gatherings. I also participated in numerous demonstrations, regardless of their sponsorship. I feel that my crossing the boundary from passively observing to actively participating was necessary for the community to feel that I was one of them. I kept myself informed of the community's activities by reading their monthly newspapers. I obtained additional data on Vietnamese immigration to France at Les Archives Nationales de France (The French National Archives).

The field techniques consisted of setting up appointments by telephone with informants, and meeting them at a place of their choice. When I was asked to choose, I usually picked a Vietnamese restaurant in the area, always taking into consideration the informant's political allegiance. The thirteenth arrondissement, for instance, was the district where I met informants who belonged to Vietnamese anticommunist organizations, because I knew that many of them were regular customers in these restaurants. On the other hand, I met informants of the pro-Hanoi faction in the fifth arrondissement, since that was their own territory. On occasion, I was invited to visit my informants in their homes. Since most of them lived in the city or in the nearby suburbs, it was often more convenient to meet them in restaurants than in their own homes.

In my interviews with my informants, I never used a tape recorder, and very seldom did I take notes during the interview. I had rejected the idea of using a tape recorder from the beginning of the fieldwork. I did not want to have on tape any information about my informants, for fear that the tapes might be stolen. I wrote down most of my notes right after the interviews, either in the bathroom of the restaurant or on the metro. I had quickly found that if I took out a piece of paper from my briefcase to write on during the interview, the discussion froze. During a long interview, I often asked for the spelling of a word. This gave me the opportunity to write down a couple of key words. Only with my best informants was I able to take notes freely.

In all, I interviewed a total of 250 Vietnamese, most of whom were members of political organizations. I met many of these people in social and cultural gatherings, and through referrals. I interviewed leaders, members, and supporters of political organizations. Two-thirds of my informants were male. Most women I interviewed belonged to the pro-Hanoi factional organizations. I met very few women who were members of the anticommunist organizations. My data does not reveal any differences between the political discourse of men and that of women.

Both men and women were among my key informants. They were the people who helped me increase my networks, whenever possible, and, most importantly, kept me informed and invited me to social activities related to their organizations. Once we developed a friendship, I saw them and phoned them regularly.

Penetrating into the Political Networks

My approach to the role of homeland politics among the Parisian Vietnamese immigrants and refugees is essentially emic, a term that implies understanding their community from their own perspective. Although the interpretation of the data is my own, I am presenting the political conflict in the community as it was explained to me by the Vietnamese themselves.

Politics is of central importance to Vietnamese immigrants and refugees in Paris, contrary to the assumption of the many French scholars who see their political activity as irrelevant. I try to present here the Vietnamese image of politics. A professor in Paris told me that the Vietnamese did not have any politics, because they did not understand what it was all about, in contrast to the French, who knew what politics was. When I shared my research project with other French scholars, I found that a number of them shared this French ethnocentric view of Vietnamese politics, and of homeland politics among immigrants. Only the French social scientists whose interests included Vietnam realized the importance of politics in the community.

As far as French Vietnamese scholars are concerned, since

they are themselves involved in this political conflict, their writings inevitably reflect their own personal political allegiances. As some of them pointed out to me, it was almost impossible for them to move freely in the two-factional network. A Vietnamese colleague in Paris told me, "Only you can do such research, because you are not Vietnamese and therefore can talk more freely about it."

This study is an attempt to understand the significance of politics for the Parisian Vietnamese and their community. The Vietnamese recognize the key role of politics in their lives, yet for them it is taboo to speak freely about the topic. For example, I once interviewed a Vietnamese scholar who told me that politics was not an important topic, yet he refused to have dinner in a Vietnamese restaurant, saying, "Let's find a place away from the community." I was told that even in family gatherings, the discussion of politics is avoided.

There is even stronger resistance to talking about politics with an outsider unfamiliar with the political situation in the community. Long-established immigrants say they experienced the infiltration of American intelligence workers during the Vietnam War, and still have not overcome their fear of strangers. At the beginning of my fieldwork, they were especially suspicious of my study since I had just come from the United States. The more recent refugees, on the other hand, were concerned about Vietnamese communist infiltration. They assumed that I was a radical American activist, since I had just come from the University of California at Berkeley. They associated Berkeley with the Vietnam antiwar movement in the 1960s. In both cases, I presented myself as a scholar who was too conspicuous to be a good spy. My argument was that the CIA or the communists did not need me to infiltrate their political networks; if they wanted to do that, they would hire a Vietnamese from the community.

I also promised my informants that I would not even try to investigate or write about covert political activities, as a security leak could seriously impair the effectiveness of the organizations. For instance, I chose not to explore politically sensitive issues such as the source of funding for the anticommunist guerrilla resistance movement, or the alleged involvement of the CIA in supporting such a movement.

After a year of intensive fieldwork, I was able to link up with both political networks. I tried to pay equal attention to both factions. I dealt with the two political factions as two units. I kept my social and cultural references from the two factions completely separate. In my discussions with informants, my discourses used only references from their own factional network, and displayed knowledge only of issues related to their own political belief. For instance, I discussed the question of "refugees" with members of the anticommunist organizations, whereas with members of the pro-Hanoi faction, I talked about the post-1975 economic situation of Vietnam.

While working within the two networks, I kept two separate address books, one for each faction's individuals and allied organizations. This practical device enabled me to avoid making any mistakes by misplacing people.

I have always made clear to all my informants the objective of the study. I never disclosed to either faction, however, any information regarding members or activities of the other. Occasionally informants attempted to pump me for information about the other faction, but I always refused to reveal anything. I knew I was in a precarious position and tried to remain impartial at all times. I also declined to participate in working on any projects. I was asked a couple of times to help write proposals for the Vietnamese community. Although there was nothing political about these projects, I knew all too well their political implications and declined to get involved on the basis of wanting to maintain my neutrality.

Upon arriving in Paris, my first task was to look into the networks that structure the Vietnamese community's life. Understanding how these networks operated was essential for this study. I learned what to ask and to whom, as well as how to formulate my own discourse accordingly. It was a technique I learned from one of my informants, who once told me that if one did not have any personal references for his or her interlocutor, one never engaged in a political discussion before finding out their political allegiance.

I discovered that the Vietnamese are bound together by two major networks, family and politics. The family network unites members of the same family regardless of individual political beliefs. In France, the family network immediately regroups after they all arrive. Often its members support themselves through family businesses. This network is very insular and private. By contrast, the political network is a looser social network made up of people who share the same political beliefs.

I was unable to utilize family or kin networks to increase my range of contacts for the study of political organizations. Since families were politically divided, one family member would not refer me to other family members who belonged to a different political faction.

Beyond family ties, the Vietnamese tend to interact with others of the same age. Since I was initially introduced to people in their twenties and thirties, I experienced difficulty obtaining introductions to older immigrants. It was six months before I established contacts with older Vietnamese immigrants. My referrals into the older community usually came from French scholars rather than from Vietnamese informants.

My first contacts in the pro-Hanoi network were given to me by Vietnamese students and faculty at the University of Paris VII. I was given names of people to interview and tips on social and cultural events and organizations to visit. I gradually established my own network in the pro-Hanoi faction. I developed friendships with my key informants and these gave me access to the community grapevine.

In contrast, I had great difficulty entering the anticommunist network. For two months, I contacted rightist French scholars and the officers of French organizations working with refugees, yet I failed to obtain any access to this network. I finally met my first informant, Nam, by going to a Tet celebration organized by the anticommunist organizations. Nam was a leader of a student organization. It was another month before he gave me further referrals. Every time I called him I had to explain the significance of my study, pointing out how important it was for his organization to participate. I remember that at one point I was so frustrated with his negative answers that I told him I could reformulate my research design to present the pro-Hanoi faction as dominant in the community. It was not too long after this incident that he gave me my second contact.

Increasing my networks in both political factions was equally difficult. I had to either find new informants on my own by going to social gatherings, or rely on my existing informants for further contacts. In some cases, I depended on my informants' willingness to give me references. I usually had to wait until they contacted possible informants before I could reach them myself. I was once given phone numbers of leaders of anticommunist organizations by one of my informants who did not want me to disclose his name to these people. When I called them, I had to make up a story about how I got their phone number. As a result, most of them refused to talk to me or see me.

The data presented here are the result of a long investigation, and are based on my accumulated knowledge rather than on my informants' disclosure of their "secrets." I gathered information wherever possible, through interviews, newspapers, or social gatherings. If a new piece of information contradicted information I had collected in a previous interview, I went back to the previous informant for an explanation. On other occasions, I tested the validity of information by using it in my own discourse during other interviews.

In addition to increasing my networks of contacts, the social and cultural gatherings turned out to be a source of information regarding my informants. Through observation, I checked out who attended the meeting and whom they knew there. It was not unusual for my key informants, who had previously phoned me about the event, not to talk to me in the presence of their friends, or they would act surprised to see me there.

As I immersed myself in the community, I adopted my informants' attitudes toward outsiders. I distrusted anyone outside the community who showed interest in my research. This became especially striking when it came to my relationship with French scholars. At the beginning of my fieldwork, I was eager to contact French scholars for support and advice, but by the end, I avoided discussing my research with them. In one instance, I met a French scholar working on Vietnam who approached me with the argument that as scholars working in the same area, we should exchange ideas and information. During our first meeting, I was vague about my research while trying to make some inferences about his political allegiance. I then phoned a friend of mine in academia for additional information regarding his politics. After learning that he had connections with Hanoi, I refused to disclose to him any information regarding the anticommunist organizations.

To other scholars and to the Vietnamese people involved in this political debate, I do not pretend to reveal here any absolute truths. The data presented and analyzed are the product of my own interpretation of situations as I experienced them and of information as it was revealed to me by informants. By presenting both factions as they presented themselves to me, I intend in this book to deepen public understanding of the conflict and to open discussion. All the names I have used in this book are fictitious to protect the identity of my informants.

Chapter 2

The Role of History in the Shaping of a Political Identity

Leaders of the pro-Hanoi and anticommunist factions of the Parisian Vietnamese community have used Vietnamese history in their political discourse as a persuasive tool to recruit new members. The leaders' discourse addresses the popular issue of Vietnamese cultural and political identity. Woodside (1976:1) argues:

> The depth of the Vietnamese people's consciousness of their own history and literature would astonish the far less imaginative nationalists and relic-worshippers of North America and of Western Europe.

Regardless of their political allegiance, Vietnamese immigrants and refugees have not only remained loyal to Vietnam but also see themselves as playing a role in Vietnamese history. Although they no longer live in Vietnam, they are aware of the impact of the overseas Vietnamese communities in recent Vietnamese history. And they regard history as more than simply a display of the past that can be contemplated as part of one's own cultural identity. Le Thanh Khoi (1955:7), a Vietnamese scholar educated in France, states in the introduction to his book on the history of Vietnam:

> . . . l'histoire n'est pas seulement la science du passé humain, elle est aussi celle de l'époque contemporaine. La

découverte du passé n'offre tout son intérêt qu'en tant qu'ex-plication du présent.[1]

The Vietnamese people's understanding of their own history in-cludes notions of both continuity and change. They evoke their common culture, and yet recognize the social and political forces that have shaped Vietnamese society. But history is also used as a tool to shape one's own political identity, through selection and interpretation of historical facts.

The discourse of both factions evokes the common theme of Vietnamese resistance to foreign domination, such as that of the Chinese and the French. There is a great discrepancy, however, between the pro-Hanoi and anticommunist factions in the way they interpret their history after the end of French colonialism and the introduction of communism in Vietnam.

The pro-Hanoi leaders argue that the Communist party was the main force behind Vietnamese independence. They blame the United States for the war and for maintaining the arbitrary divi-sion of Vietnamese territory. After the fall of Saigon in 1975, these leaders described Vietnam as an independent country, liberated from American imperialism. The pro-Hanoi leaders and intellec-tuals claim that Vietnamese communism embodies Vietnamese culture, whereas the anticommunists see it as a foreign, external ideology.

The anticommunist leaders portray the Vietnamese com-munist leaders as Soviet puppets who have little interest in preserving the national identity of Vietnam. They recognized the weaknesses of the South Vietnamese government during the Viet-nam War, but blame the Americans for its 1975 defeat on the grounds that the United States did not give it sufficient support. Leaders of the anticommunist faction depict Vietnam today as a country ruled by a totalitarian regime controlled by the Soviet Union. They claim that the Vietnamese people under communism have not only lost their freedom, but are also losing their cultural identity.

---

1. . . . . history is knowledge not only of the human past, but also of contemporary times. The discovery of the past offers its full interest only when it explains the present.

Vietnamese history has been studied principally by Vietnamese, French, and American scholars. All these scholars have used history as a means to unravel the complexity of the Vietnamese wars, which were then subject to interpretation. These studies reflect the political biases of their respective authors, their national affiliations, personal involvements, firsthand experience of the conflicts, and the political climate during which their work was published.

Questions of truth and history are still heated issues in reconstructing the historical facts regarding Vietnam. During the Vietnam War, the conflict spilled over the geographical boundaries of Vietnam and divided the United States into two opposing political camps over the issue of American interventionist policies in Vietnam. Since American bureaucrats, intellectuals, and journalists were themselves actors in the American political arena, their representations of the Vietnamese conflict have portrayed two versions of reality. A "reality" implies having a perception of truth. A historical event, for instance, is a fact that generates a number of perceived truths according to the actor's own representation of the event itself and his or her interpretation of it within a specific political framework of analysis. The scholarly study of Vietnamese history thus presents a double reality, because it reflects the two political discourses: one procommunist and against American involvement; the other anticommunist and favoring American intervention.

A few years ago, journalist Stanley Karnow's PBS television series entitled "Vietnam: A Television History" sparked fervent political arguments regarding the accuracy or biases of the documentary. In *Losers Are Pirates*, a book financed by American Vietnamese refugee organizations as a fund-raising effort within the community, James Banerian, a free-lance writer, criticizes Karnow for lacking objectivity in his presentation of Vietnamese history, and for giving inaccurate information (Banerian 1985:i). He claims to present in his own book the "truth" from people who have a "knowledgeable eye" (Banerian 1985). His informants are Vietnamese refugees who fled Vietnam after 1975 and whose political identity is anticommunist. The refugees' interpretation of history thus reflects only anticommunist Vietnamese political discourse. Banerian (1985:i) assesses Karnow's series thus:

The program seemed to be an irregular mixture of clichés and one-sided memories, causing consultant Douglas Pike to conclude: "Whatever this thing is, it is not history."

In his own writing, however, Banerian uses the other set of political biases and clichés regarding the Vietnamese communists, and in particular Ho Chi Minh. He states (1985:71):

These clever images almost make us forget that Ho's hero was Josef Stalin and that his policies are responsible for the deaths of millions of people all over Indochina.

This example illustrates how history can be reconstructed based on another political discourse that derives from the writer's own political allegiance. Alleged truth is thus constructed from political discourses. "Truth" is produced within political discourses that are in themselves neither true nor false (Foucault 1980).

A critical analysis of all studies on the history of Vietnam is beyond the scope of this chapter. I propose instead to focus on selected historical facts that I will argue have shaped Vietnamese political identity, and therefore the political conflict among the Vietnamese overseas communities, taking into consideration various interpretations.

Vietnam and China: A Question of Identity

Vietnamese culture has much in common with the cultures of other Southeast Asian peoples, yet Vietnam contrasts sharply with its neighbors as a result of a thousand years of Chinese domination, the impact of which has indeed shaped Vietnam's economics, politics, and culture. In contrast to peoples in other Chinese provinces, however, the Vietnamese were never totally assimilated into the Chinese empire. Throughout history, the Vietnamese people have been open to foreign ideas, yet fiercely resistant to any foreign domination. Foreigners have been paradoxically both a threat to Vietnamese political autonomy, and a source of new ideas.

Marr (1971:8) argues that the Vietnamese have tended to define themselves in contrast to their neighbors: they typically differentiated themselves both from the highland people they called

Montagnards, who do not practice wet-rice cultivation, and from the Khmer, wet-rice cultivators who "did not share their choices of house structures, familial and village organization, and forms of religious observance." Marr suggests that the Vietnamese believed their relationships with these groups would not threaten their identity, whereas their relationship with their powerful neighbor China did confront them with a problem of identity. "The difficulty comes in conveying the subtle interplay of resistance and dependence which appeared often to stand at the root of historical Vietnamese attitudes toward the Chinese" (Marr 1971:9).

Vietnamese scholars trace the origin of Vietnamese cultural identity to the people of the Red River Delta. Le Thanh Khoi (1955), for instance, attributes Vietnamese cultural identity to a fusion of Southeast Asian and Mongolitic languages, physical traits, and cultural practices centuries before the Christian era. He contends that the Lac civilization (207 B.C.) shaped Vietnamese identity and constituted the origin of Vietnamese ethnicity. The Lac Viet, also called Lo Yue by the Chinese, lived in small villages at the Red River Delta in northern Vietnam. The Lac civilization was characterized by an economy based on wet-rice cultivation, by a chiefdom controlled by members of noble families with religious, military, and civil power, and by the practices of body tattooing and betel nut chewing (1955).

Under ten centuries of Chinese domination, however, Vietnamese society was reshaped according to the Chinese model. Confucianism and Taoism were the most important cultural traits adopted by the Vietnamese. While Confucianism as a philosophy dictates all social and political relationships within and outside the family, Taoism outlines principles for a universal harmony. Many Vietnamese as well as Western scholars acknowledged this fusion of the indigenous cultural traits of the Red River Delta people with institutions and cultural values borrowed from China, and referred to it as the traditional Vietnamese identity (Woodside 1971).

Although Vietnamese society was strongly influenced by China, the Vietnamese people always perceived themselves as a culturally distinct ethnic group. They simply refused to be assimilated into the Chinese empire. The first act of Vietnamese resistance to the Chinese invaders was in the first century, a military insurrection led by the two Trung sisters (Le Thanh Khoi 1955;

Woodside 1971). These women became legendary national heroines. Le Thanh Khoi (1955) suggests that this rebellion became a model for the Vietnamese people, helping them strengthen their national identity. Huynh Kim Khanh (1982:33), however, provides another interpretation: "The resistance to China was essentially an effort to retain political autonomy vis-à-vis a vastly more powerful neighbor . . . Questions of race, culture and ideology remained peripheral."

Under French colonialism, the Vietnamese resistance movements emerged from a more complex set of sociopolitical relationships. The emergence of "nationalist movements" is still a subject for argument among scholars. Marr (1971) points out that "petit bourgeois" Vietnamese intellectuals adopted the concept "nationalism" only in the 1920s. These intellectuals labeled Vietnam's resistance to foreign intervention as "nationalism," based on a modern concept of the nation-state, one that Vietnamese scholars used as a positive dynamic ideology.

Vietnamese resistance to successive foreign interventions, Chinese and French, was in fact generated by "patriotism," *ai quoc*, rather than by "nationalism." Vietnamese "patriotism" is a concept that deals more with ethnic and cultural-linguistic boundaries than with national and territorial ones (Huynh Kim Khanh 1982; Marr 1971).

With the independence of Vietnam from China in 974, political conflict emerged among the ruling Vietnamese families. Regional warlords frequently challenged the authority of the monarchs and tried to usurp their power. In the longest conflict, which lasted for three centuries, the Mac and the Trinh families in the North, who claimed to be the protectors of the Le dynasty, opposed the Nguyen warlords, who ruled in the South. In 1802, the country was reunited under Nguyen Anh, later called Gia Long, an heir of the Nguyen rulers. To successfully gain military control over Vietnam, Gia Long called upon the French as advisors. Since sixteen hundred the French missionaries, who were already active in Vietnam, had asked France for assistance in helping Gia Long gain full military power over Vietnam. Gia Long also looked to China for a political model that would secure his power. He created the first Vietnamese dynasty in the image of the Chinese dynasty, underpinned by the principles of Confucian doctrine.

In the scholarly literature, the precolonial period is referred to as the Vietnamese tradition, and this concept has been used to oppose the Westernization and modernization brought into Vietnam by colonialism. Precolonial Vietnam is characterized by two traditions, the first being identified as the "Great Tradition," or the elite culture of the monarchy and the mandarins, and the second as the "Little Tradition," recognized as the cultures behind the "bamboo hedges" of the villages. In the process of modernization under colonial rule, the introduction of Western ideologies brought social changes to both these "traditions." There is general consensus among Vietnamese scholars and leaders that in "modern Vietnam," social reforms of the political apparatus represented by the royal court were inevitable. The emperor and mandarins in twentieth-century Vietnam, for instance, lost their political power, and this led to the decline of the "Great Tradition." The representations of the emperors' and mandarins' Confucian ethics, however, persisted. The qualities of a good leader remained the ones associated with Confucian morality. A Confucian is a self-cultivated man who is able to fulfill his obligations, and conducts himself with right behavior and respect for others. The popularity of a leader is based on his Confucian qualities. The Vietnamese communists and noncommunists still legitimate their own political power with respect to the Confucian tradition. The scholar Nguyen Khac Vien (1974:47), who was a supporter of the Vietnamese revolution, states:

> Marxism hardly came as a shock to the Confucian scholar who had always considered the highest aim of man to be the fulfillment of his social obligations . . . He is never actually hostile to the principle of collective discipline (as is the bourgeois intellectual) since he always sees social discipline as an indispensable part of the development of his own personality.

Similar arguments have been used about leaders by their supporters. Each side jealously defended the claim that their own leader was a Confucian man, and accused the other side's leader of being a self-interested individual, manipulated by foreigners. For example, in 1949 the French government tried to reinstall the emperor Bao Dai into power. By then the Vietnamese monarchy

v lost its credibility and power in Vietnam. Bao Dai did
e support of most anticolonial political groups because
Confucian stature as a leader. He was in fact consid-
puppet of the French colonial regime. Vietnamese communists and supporters argued that Ho Chi Minh was a Confucian man, even while the anticommunists accused him of being a
communist puppet of the Soviet Union.

The impact of colonialism on village life is still a subject of
argument among scholars. Vietnamese scholars who supported
the Vietnamese revolution, like Le Thanh Khoi, Nguyen Khac
Vien, and Phan Thi Dac, stress in their writing the negative impact modernization has had on village life. They argue, for instance, that colonialism introduced the villages to the Western
concept of individualism associated with capitalism. Phan Thi Dac
(1966) suggests that in the traditional Vietnamese village a moral
solidarity existed among people, and that the notion of individualism was a product of French colonialism. Le Thanh Khoi (1955)
also argues that the introduction of capitalist modes of production
that favored individualism into the Vietnamese village has
weakened social and familial ties among Vietnamese peasants.

Some Western scholars like Popkin (1979) disagree with
those Vietnamese scholars who believe that colonial administrative decrees changing the traditional methods for selecting village
notables and chiefs destroyed the villagers' sense of collective obligation and mutual support. He argues that the villages of North
Vietnam (Tonkin) and central Vietnam (Annam) remained corporate until World War II. The old village elite manipulated the
decrees to their own advantage. In Cochin China or South Vietnam, since there was little or no sense of local citizenship and no
elaborate internal ranking system, the French were able to consoli-
date villages (Popkin 1979:141).

French Colonialism and the Early Vietnamese
Anticolonial Movements

French colonialism did not have the same impact on Vietnamese
society as Chinese domination in the earliest period did. The
French colonial experience reveals a cultural clash that derived
from the ideology of domination and subordination inherent in

colonialism. Yacono (1973:18) summarizes the principles of colonialism as follows:

> Assimilation, sujétion, autonomie, trois lignes de force qu'on retrouve dans l'organisation administrative comme dans les structures de l'économie coloniale, l'esprit de domination constituant la dominante avec le souci du contrôle et la subordination aux intérêts de la métropole.[2]

The notion of domination, which justified the actions of the European nations in building their colonial empires, was based on a nineteenth-century European faith in progress and the moral superiority of the white man. It was indeed believed that colonialism would bring a better and more civilized life for the "native people" (Osborne 1969:33). Colonialism was viewed by the French as a humanitarian act, the so-called mission civilisatrice.

Under French colonialism, Vietnam was geographically and politically divided into three different regions. North Vietnam, or Tonkin, and central Vietnam, or Annam, were converted into "protectorates" under a colonial policy known as an "association," which permitted the coexistence of new institutions with the old ones (Woodside 1976:3). At Hue, for instance, the Vietnamese monarchy and its bureaucracy survived and operated in a circumscribed and subordinate manner (Woodside 1976:3). South Vietnam, or Cochin China, Cambodia, and Laos were ruled as a full colony under the control of one "governor-General."

McAlister (1969) argues that colonialism reinforced regionalism not only because of the difference in administration, but also due to social and economic changes. He states (1969:43) that

> industrial development in the north, and plantation agriculture along with a vast increase in cultivable land in the Mekong Delta in the south produced conspicuous regional peculiarities in Vietnamese society.

---

2. Assimilation, subjection, autonomy—the three principles driving both the administrative bureaucracy and the structures of the colonial economy, the main concept being domination to control everything and subordinate it to the interests of the mother country.

For instance, French hydraulic engineering made the salty land of the Mekong Delta suitable for cultivation. This land was sold to large landowners "as a means of rapidly recouping the cost of the projects," but this created the basis for the agrarian problems that were to follow (McAlister and Mus 1970:80). McAlister and Mus (1970:82) assert that opening new land for cultivation created not only a new class of wealthy landowners but also a rootless peasantry. Another consideration was the fact that village customs and family structures in the south were more informal and less rigid than in the north. McAlister (1969:44) concludes: "These characteristics have made the southerners more amenable to change."

French colonialism hastened the decline of the Vietnamese bureaucracy. "The Confucian bureaucracy remained the most important organized segment of Vietnamese society to feel the full impact of colonialism" (Woodside 1976:16). The Vietnamese bureaucracy of course had begun to decay long before French intervention, but this process was accelerated under colonialism. Woodside suggests that the bureaucracy lost its sense of collective identity when the ritualized classical examination was abolished in 1919 and new recruits were no longer indoctrinated for professional service. Under French colonialism, the mandarins found themselves in competition with French civil servants, who were better paid than they. They accepted bribes in order to maintain a dignified life-style. Due to this corruption, the Vietnamese bureaucrats lost their credibility among the indigenous population (Popkin 1979:134).

As a result, new social groups emerged under French colonialism. Woodside (1971:9) reports that these new groups were raised "to great heights by a new kind of social mobility which involved the arbitrary redistribution of influence and power." The French administration created a new Vietnamese middle class. They were recruited on "a 'non-ascriptive' basis of which applicant possessed the most personal merit and talent" (Woodside 1976:9).

The Vietnamese resistance to French colonialism began with the establishment of colonial rule in 1858 (Marr 1971; Woodside 1976). Although resistance to foreign domination already existed in Vietnam, it burned "with an especially bright flame" during the earliest French invasion (Woodside 1976:29). According to my informants in both factions, there was a general consensus to get rid of the French.

In the beginning, these movements were oriented toward reinstating into power the Vietnamese monarchy and the mandarins of precolonial Vietnam (Buttinger 1972; Marr 1971; Woodside 1976). The last movement of this kind, the Can Vuong (Loyalty to the King), led by the scholar-gentry, rejected all forms of social change brought in by colonialism. By 1897 the Can Vuong movement was no longer in existence. Marr contends that this movement was a mass movement led by the scholar-gentry class, whose "leaders mobilized the local peasantry more for common soldiering and logistical backup than for the provision of comprehensive intelligence of the enemy or impressive political response and support" (Marr 1971:76).

But by the turn of the century, the emergence of a new anticolonial movement led by the scholar Phan Boi Chau set a precedent for the anticolonial movement. First of all the resistance movement was carried out both in Vietnam and in Vietnamese overseas communities. Sons of mandarins who were fighting colonialism went abroad to be educated in China and Japan. Other leaders who went into exile sought out foreign ideologies that might be useful to fight colonialism and "modernize" Vietnam. Like his predecessors of the Can Vuong movement, Phan Boi Chau was committed to the idea of restoring the monarchy, but he also believed in social change in Vietnam. Inspired by Japan's anticolonial movement, he wanted to radically modernize Vietnam under the leadership of a progressive emperor. Traveling in Japan and China, Chau united a number of Vietnamese emigrant nationalist groups into a League for the Restoration of Vietnam. "He called for students to follow him overseas, spoke more feelingly of the value of propaganda in the slow process of building national unity" (Marr 1971:130).

The Vietnamese overseas in China, Japan, and France in the early twentieth century played a major role in the Vietnamese anticolonial movements. In Vietnam any uprising was systematically suppressed by the French colonial administration. Although tracked by the *Sureté* (French police), Vietnamese anticolonial leaders abroad enjoyed more freedom to carry out their political activities and were able to gain support from foreign political parties.

The Vietnamese revolution began to grow during the mid-1920s (Woodside 1976:59). This revolutionary movement was led by a new generation of intellectuals referred to as the intelligentsia, *gioi tria thuc* (Marr 1981). Unlike the scholar-gentry class, this new intelligentsia was ironically a product of the colonial system. They had graduated from French and Franco-Vietnamese schools, and understood "the Neo-Confucian classics only vaguely but were impatient to digest two millennia of European learning in a matter of a few years" (Marr 1981:9). Even though some of them held high positions in the colonial administration, these intellectuals were disenchanted with the colonial apparatus and ended up opposing the French.

The Vietnamese Nationalist party, Viet Nam Quoc Dan Dang, also referred to as the VNQDD, was founded in 1927 in Tonkin under the leadership of Nguyen Thai Hoc, with the nationalist intelligentsia at its core. According to Woodside (1976), the Nationalist party set a new stage for the Vietnamese revolution because it represented a variety of social groups. The VNQDD represented the vestige of Vietnamese elite nationalism, and not only was responsible for armed uprisings in cities, but even attacked French-occupied military centers. After the VNQDD sponsored a mutiny of Vietnamese troops at the Yen Bay garrison, the French colonial government retaliated by arresting and killing most of its leaders, including Nguyen Thai Hoc. Remnants of the VNQDD who went into exile in China continued to be active in Vietnamese politics, in collaboration with the Kuomintang in the 1940s and with the United States in the 1960s (Huynh Kim Khanh 1982:99).

The introduction of communism into the anticolonial movements marked the beginning of a deeper split in the Vietnamese political arena, from which emerged three distinct political forces: the Marxist-Leninist and Stalinist communists, the Trotskyists, and the noncommunist nationalists. Although the internal unity of each group was often threatened by political factionalism, their disagreements remained within the core ideology of the group. In the Parisian Vietnamese community, for example, both the pro-Hanoi and the anticommunist factions endure conflict within their organizations, but each group remains committed to its own political ideology.

The Vietnamese Revolution and the Division of Vietnam

The leader of the Vietnamese communist revolution was Nguyen Tat Thanh, best known by his last two pseudonyms, Nguyen Ai Quoc and Ho Chi Minh. For the Vietnamese communists and their supporters, Ho Chi Minh was the father of the Vietnamese revolution who championed all other Vietnamese anticolonial political groups to successfully win Vietnamese independence and bring social reform into a feudal Vietnamese society. His devotion to his country made him a true Vietnamese leader whose political morality was that of a Confucian man (Huynh Kim Khanh 1982; Le Thanh Khoi 1955; Nguyen Khac Vien 1974). Truong Nhu Tang, a former Vietcong, recalled in his memoir (1986:16) after having met Ho Chi Minh that he was "Nationalist, Humanist, Marxist-Leninist, Machiavellian, Confucian — these were just some of the aspects of his remarkable character." For the Vietnamese anticommunists, on the other hand, Ho Chi Minh was a revolutionary who played the nationalists' game, but devoted himself to the cause of international communism rather than to Vietnamese independence (Hoang Van Chi 1964).

Ho Chi Minh lived abroad for more than twenty years, residing in a number of countries, among them France, the Soviet Union, and China. "The search for teachers, techniques, and material assistance for decolonization became a search for new values and an institutional system that would not only help Vietnam regain its independence but also revitalize Vietnamese society" (Huynh Kim Khanh 1982:54). In Canton in 1925, Ho Chi Minh created the Vietnam Thanh Nien Kach Menh Hoi, also called Thanh Nien (Vietnamese Revolutionary Youth Association), an organization that marked the beginning of Vietnamese communism. The Thanh Nien was different from all earlier anticolonial organizations because it emphasized the importance of a revolutionary theory (Huynh Kim Khanh 1982). Thanh Nien's outlines of the revolution focused on the people most oppressed by the colonial regime: the peasants and workers (Huynh Kim

Khanh 1982). The outlines said that Vietnamese intellectuals and members of the bourgeoisie who are least exploited have to ally themselves with the masses for the liberation of the country. At the First National Party Congress of Thanh Nien in 1929, Thanh Nien collapsed as a united anticolonial political organization, when three factional communist organizations emerged (Huynh Kim Khanh 1982). The leaders of these communist organizations, themselves former Thanh Nien leaders, competed for the leadership of the Vietnamese communist organizations.

In 1930, Ho Chi Minh founded the first united communist party, the Indochinese Communist party (Hemery 1975; Huynh Kim Khanh 1982; Le Thanh Khoi 1955). The Indochinese Communist party gained increasing support from among the workers and small peasants between 1930 and 1945, when Vietnam was afflicted by the worldwide depression of the 1930s (Chesneaux 1955; Woodside 1976) that caused a slump in overseas trade and a sharp drop in the prices of rice, rubber, and coal, and therefore in people's living standards (Woodside 1976:173).

Ho Chi Minh's concept of revolution was based on two principles, patriotism and devotion to the cause of internationalism: "He favored the direct intervention of the international Communist movement in the national liberation movement of 'the East' and collaboration between the proletariat of Europe and the national liberationists of the colonies" (Huynh Kim Khanh 1982:61). Ho Chi Minh organized the Vietnamese revolution in accordance with the early Marxist concept of class struggle and Lenin's notion of imperialism. Ho Chi Minh viewed French colonialism as a direct consequence of imperialism. In his essay "Indochina and the Pacific," Ho Chi Minh wrote that "capitalism now uses one colony as a tool for exploiting another; this is the case of Indochina and the Pacific area" (Ho Chi Minh 1967:31). After World War I, the international Marxist movement recognized nationalist movements in colonized countries as new forces to fight capitalism.

In the history of the Vietnamese revolutionary movement, the conflict between the Vietnamese Stalinists and Trotskyists remains a bitter memory for Vietnamese Trotskyists living in France. From 1933 to 1937 in South Vietnam, a "united front," whose leadership included both Stalinists and Trotskyists, formed a group called La Lutte (The Struggle), which was named after their newspaper *La Lutte*. Their short alliance resulted in their members' winning their most notable election, to the Municipal Council of Saigon and the Colonial Council of Cochin China (Huynh Kim Khanh 1982; Le Thanh Khoi 1955). The Vietnamese Trotskyists, who followed Trotsky's concept of class struggle and anti-imperialism, fielded a worker slate composed of intellectuals and workers (Huynh Kim Khanh 1982). They accused the Vietnamese Stalinists of following Stalin, who was responsible for the deaths of millions of people, and accused the Marxist-Leninist communists led by Ho Chi Minh of betraying the interests of the proletariat. In 1939 under colonial repression in South Vietnam, most of the Stalinist, Marxist-Leninist and Trotskyist Vietnamese leaders were imprisoned. But in 1945 after their liberation, the Vietnamese Stalinists launched a major reprisal against the Trotskyists, and assassinated most of their leaders.

In 1941, during World War II, Ho Chi Minh founded the Viet Nam Doc Lap Dong Minh, also called the Vietminh Front, which, according to Huynh Kim Khanh (1982:264), was not a political party, but rather an organizational front of the Indochinese Communist party. The objective of the Vietminh Front was to attract into its fight against the enemy all anticolonial elements of Vietnamese society, including workers, peasants, and members of all other social classes. From 1940 to 1945 both the French and the Japanese were considered enemies of the Vietnamese revolution (Huynh Kim Khanh 1982). The Vietminh Front adopted the strategy of insurrection borrowed from the Chinese People's Liberation Army. Introducing the guerrilla armed forces contributed to the Vietnamese revolution.

French colonialism ended with the Geneva Agreement of 1954, after the French army was defeated by Vietminh forces at Dien Bien Phu. Vietnam was then divided into two countries at the seventeenth parallel: North Vietnam as the Democratic Republic of Vietnam under the leadership of Ho Chi Minh, and South Vietnam as the Republic of Vietnam under the leadership of Ngo Dinh Diem. The 1954 agreement also called for a general election in Vietnam, which would have taken place in 1956 but was repudiated by Diem. This arbitrary division of Vietnam was not based on regional or cultural differences between the north and the south, but rather was a political division opposing the com-

munist regime in the north to a series of anticommunist governments in the south. After 1954, most of the southern Vietminh
forces moved north, and most northern Vietnamese Catholics
resettled in the south. Most of the leaders of the northern
Democratic Republic of Vietnam were in fact from central Vietnam, which under the 1954 agreement was excluded as a region
and integrated into South Vietnam (Brocheux and Hemery 1980).

The subsequent American intervention in Vietnam was
aimed at guiding the South Vietnamese government in building
a democratic country in the image of the West, and at preventing
the spread of communism to other Southeast Asian countries
(Fitzgerald 1973; Kahin 1987; Patti 1982). For the next twenty
years, American involvement gradually escalated from military
advisors to American armed forces. The first Indochinese war had
ended with the French troops' departure from South Vietnam in
1955 and the second Vietnam war began with the arrival of American troops in South Vietnam. Over the next twenty years, American deployment of sophisticated modern warfare technology
against Vietnamese peasants on bicycles (Gibson 1988:17) brought
the Vietnamese conflict to worldwide attention. The Tet Offensive
of 1968, led by the Vietminh and Vietcong forces below the seventeenth parallel, marked a turning point in the history of the Vietnam War. The wide coverage of the battle in the American press
"had an electrifying effect on popular opinion in the United States"
(Fitzgerald 1973:525). Before 1968, the Johnson administration
had wanted the American people to believe that American victory
was inevitable (Gibson 1988). In the wake of the uncertainty of
American victory, and the full-scale warfare already under way in
Vietnam, the American people became divided over America's involvement in Vietnam. After 1968, the Nixon administration intensified the war to suppress the Vietcong forces in the south, and
retaliated against North Vietnam, but the antiwar and the peace
movements of the late 1960s intensified. In South Vietnam and
abroad, Vietnamese intellectuals also took part in the antiwar
movement. In South Vietnam after the Tet Offensive, the Alliance
of National, Democratic and Peace Forces, also called the Third
Force, became more active; it had been created in 1965 as a result
of American armed forces intervention in Vietnam. "The offensive
had pointed toward a future of even greater and more pervasive

violence" (Truong Nhu Tang 1986). Although a noncommunist political organization, the Third Force formed a partnership with the National Liberation Front in South Vietnam, also called NLF. According to Truong Nhu Tang (1986), members of the Third Force allied with the NLF because of personal relationships and family loyalty. Such an alliance was based on the Confucian concept of faithfulness, one of the basic ethical principles of the Confucian philosophy.

During the American Vietnam War, the two main opponents in the south were the political and military forces of the South Vietnamese government, or the GVN, supported by the United States, and those of the NLF, also called the Vietcong, supported by the Democratic Republic of Vietnam (North).

For the Vietnamese anticommunists, Ngo Dinh Diem remains a major political figure in the history of Vietnam. He was a fervent nationalist strongly opposed to both the French colonialists and the Vietnamese communists. They attribute Diem's fall to his personality rather than his politics. Manh, a seventy-year-old doctor who was Diem's prime minister in 1954, recalls Diem as being an honest man but impossible to work with. Manh resigned from his position ten months after he was appointed. He comments that Diem was unable to take advice from others or use them to his advantage. According to Manh, Diem distrusted anyone other than members of his own family. The Vietnamese communists and pro-Hanoi supporters accuse Diem of being an old-fashioned mandarin who remained in the service of French colonialism, fighting Marxism bitterly. "Ngo Dinh Diem was one of the most zealous servants of the colonial regime during the repression which started in 1930" (Nguyen Khac Vien 1974:46).

Like many others among the Vietnamese intelligentsia, Diem, born of a Catholic family, was educated in French and classical Chinese (Fall 1963:235). Diem advocated resistance against both French colonialism and Vietnamese communism. On a number of occasions, he turned down appointment as the prime minister of Bao Dai's government, a post that he did hold for a very short period. He accused the emperor of being "nothing but an instrument in the hands of the French authority" (Duncanson 1968). In 1945 while a prisoner of the Vietminh, he also refused Ho Chi

Minh's invitation to join the Vietnamese Communist party; he held Ho Chi Minh responsible for the assassination of his brother Ngo Dinh Khoi (Fall 1963, Duncanson 1968). Like other Vietnamese anticolonialist leaders, Ngo Dinh Diem left Vietnam in 1950, only to return four years later. He traveled to Japan, the United States, and Europe, where he looked for support among the Vietnamese overseas anticolonial organizations and sought advice and support from foreign political parties (Fall 1963:243).

In 1955, Diem held and won the first Vietnamese election in the south, which transformed the monarchy into a republic with himself as the new head of state. As a fervent anticommunist, Diem gained the support of the American government.

> Despite his rigidity, his penchant for a one-man show, and his inability to communicate or deal with people, Diem was a nationalist, untainted by past association with either the Viet-Minh or the French. (Patti 1982:443)

Although Diem used American military support, he also refused to become a puppet of the United States. Diem's political ideas were strongly influenced by both Catholicism and Confucianism. For instance, Diem adopted the political philosophy of Personalism, which was developed in the post-Depression 1930s by Emmanuel Mounier, the leader of a group of young Catholics (Fall 1963). "Personalism presumably emphasizes human dignity or the value of humanism in modern society, in contrast to Communism's treatment of the human being as merely a subcomponent of the 'masses' " (Fall 1963:247). Yet Diem believed that socioeconomic development should precede political freedom. The people, for instance, should rely on the leadership of the elite in accordance with Confucian doctrine. Surrounded in his government by family members, Diem ruled as an emperor (Duncanson 1968).

Diem's policies were directly aimed at suppressing Vietnamese communist infiltration in the south. He had also made other enemies. Among them were southern nationalist and former anticolonialist groups such as the politico-religious sects the Hoa Hao, the Cao Dai, and the Binh Xuyen, as well as the Buddhists, who opposed his regime because of its favoritism toward Catholics

(Fall 1963:245). The Buddhist monks, becoming leaders of the opposition to the regime, condemned the secret police, corruption, arbitrary arrests, and terror. The self-immolation of the monk Thich Quang Duc in June 1963 gave impetus to Buddhist protest movements. Diem's political career ended with his assassination in 1963.

The NLF was one of the most vigilant groups in opposition to Diem and to later South Vietnamese governments. For many Vietnamese anticommunists, the NLF consisted of Vietnamese communists from the north and was an organization essentially controlled by the communist regime in Hanoi. Truong Nhu Tang (1986) argues in contrast that the NLF was a southern-based revolutionary organization that in the late 1960s became dominated by the leadership of Hanoi. By that time the NLF had become more and more dependent on northern military aid. The NLF had been formally created in 1960, although the movement was already in existence three years earlier (Truong Nhu Tang 1986). Until 1962 the "hard core" of the NLF belonged to the Marxist-Leninist party; after the Congress of 1962, they had included in the party a number of South Vietnamese intellectuals who were opposed to Diem and to American intervention in Vietnam. The NLF as a southern communist revolutionary organization proposed a unified Vietnam on the basis of mutual interests between North and South Vietnam. The NLF was strongly supported among the peasants. In 1969 the NLF called for a government in the south, the Provisional Revolutionary Government, which provided a political platform for the NLF. After 1975, the NLF leaders were replaced by Hanoi-backed leaders from the north (Brocheux and Hemery 1980; Truong Nhu Tang 1986).

For the next twelve years the Republic of (South) Vietnam was governed by a succession of military leaders, among them General Duong Van Minh, General Nguyen Khanh, Air Vice Marshal Nguyen Cao Ky, and General Nguyen Van Thieu, the first and last elected president of South Vietnam after the fall of Diem's government. These leaders had received good military training but no training in political leadership (Woodside 1976). Woodside argues that the army in South Vietnam operated almost under Confucian doctrine, stressing the ethics of family solidarity. The army indeed became the channel for upward mobility, and army families took as much pride in the success of their sons in the army as the gentry families had when their sons passed the examinations in precolonial Vietnam (Woodside 1976). Although Vietnamese army officers behaved like mandarins, Confucianism as a philosophy was not used as a moral code within the army. Serving in the army was a contribution to the family honor. Woodside argues that the South Vietnamese army was doomed to defeat because it lacked any positive universal or national ideology and could not survive on the battlefield without American military backing. The unpopular American-backed government leaders provoked widespread discontent among the Vietnamese population (Woodside 1976:281).

The withdrawal of American troops in 1973 left the South Vietnamese military forces in a weak position vis-à-vis the well-equipped, better organized North Vietnamese troops. Thieu's government surrendered to the Vietnamese communist troops in April 1975. While leaders of the NLF, the Provisional Revolutionary Government (PRG), and the Third Force in the south welcomed the liberation of South Vietnam, they were disappointed when they were replaced by northern communist cadres (Truong Nhu Tang 1986).

The Reunification of Vietnam

The political conflict between Vietnamese communists and non-communists did not end with the reunification of Vietnam. While the Vietnamese communists have gained political power in South Vietnam, former South Vietnamese government members and their supporters have gone into exile. In countries such as the United States, France, Canada, and Australia, where a million Vietnamese refugees have resettled, the anticommunist organizations have formed international overseas political networks. A number of Vietnamese intellectuals and politicians who fought for peace in South Vietnam and against the corrupt Saigon governments welcomed the Vietnamese communist takeover in 1975. But in practice the communist regime, once installed in South Vietnam, fell far short of reaching their expectations of a new and free society. Disappointed and frustrated, many of them went into exile (Truong Nhu Tang 1986; Viet Tran 1979).

The extent to which a Marxist-Leninist communism has been implemented in Vietnamese society is still a matter of political debate and interpretation. Le Thanh Khoi (1978) suggests that socialism will have to remodel Vietnamese culture but keep its essence. He argues that while the Vietnamese cultural heritage ought to be preserved, new ideologies from the socialist revolution should be integrated to form a new image of Vietnam. He states:

> Ce patrimoine que nous préconisons d'assimiler d'une façon critique nous plait non seulement par sa forme nationale, mais encore par son humanisme qui contribue à enrichir notre humanisme socialiste moderne. (Le Thanh Khoi 1978:293)[3]

Le Thanh Khoi, like many other Vietnamese scholars now living abroad who have supported the Vietnamese revolution, tends to portray Vietnam as an ideal socialist country but refuses to criticize the Vietnamese Communist party.

Huynh Kim Khanh (1982:338) asserted that while the grafting of Marxism-Leninism in Vietnamese society has already taken place, "indigenization" had yet to begin. For many Vietnamese leaders of anticommunist organizations, the so-called indigenization is not about to take place in Vietnam. According to Vietnamese refugee informants who have left Vietnam over the last ten years, the Vietnamese people have not converted to the communist ideology but rather have resigned themselves to their own fate.

Socialist reforms have been implemented in North Vietnam since 1954, under war circumstances. When similar social reforms were imposed in the south after 1975, they met great resistance. The New Economic Zones created by the government to deal with unemployment in urban areas and to remedy the deficiency in food production are a good example of the unpopularity of some of the social reforms in the south. The purpose of this program was to displace thousands of urban dwellers to the countryside to help

---

3. We recommend critically assimilating this patrimony, for not only its national but also its humanistic aspect, which will contribute to the enlargement of our modern socialist humanism.

with food production (Condominas and Pottier 1982:104). According to a number of my informants in Hong Kong, San Francisco, and Paris, people who had lived in the New Economic Zones, these new zones were often removed from "civilization," as one of my informants puts it. In the new zones, they were forced to work long hours in poor sanitary conditions, suffering from lack of food and poor management. For many of those I interviewed, the New Economic Zones, although less harsh than the reeducation camps, were used to punish people who had enjoyed a better life under the former South Vietnamese regime.

French scholars like Brocheux, Hemery, and Boudarel attribute the failure of socialist reform in South Vietnam to the Vietnamese communist bureaucracy, a model of control borrowed from the West. Brocheux and Hemery (1980:15) describe it as:

> . . . monopolisation du pouvoir dans une structure bureaucratique aux mains d'une couche de "cadres," insertion dans un système d'alliances, inter-étatiques extérieures qui a achevé au Vietnam ce qui était, au départ, un vaste mouvement national et social riche et diversifié, porteur d'innombrables possibilités autres.[4]

Boudarel (1983), in his essay on the bureaucracy in Vietnam, strongly criticizes the imposition of a socialist identity. The Vietnamese version of the Chinese communist bureaucracy is based on an ideology that reinforces the collectivism of the Party members, the cadres. The *chinh huan* is a method of "reform-instruction" whereby the cadres are forced to reevaluate their political ideology through self-criticism. Boudarel (1983:60–61) notes the aims of this method:

> Changer les idées, la conscience et les moeurs, tel est le moteur et le but du système. On n'a donc pas affaire à un enseignement visant à ouvrir les esprits, mais à une opération

---

4. Centralization of power in a bureaucratic structure controlled by a few cadres, integration into an alliance system with foreign nations, which has destroyed in Vietnam what was at the beginning a large national and social movement, rich and diverse, carrying countless other possiblities.

de remodelage du caractère, du tempérament, des idées, en bref de toute la psychologie de l'hômme. Le but n'est pas intellectuel, mais affectif: créer une nouvelle mentalité, un nouveau comportement.[5]

According to Boudarel, this method has been overused by Party members since the death of Ho Chi Minh. It is no longer a matter of political discussion about the individual's political ideology, but rather a public humiliation and a brainwashing that forces individuals to conform to the collective behavior dictated by the state. Boudarel (1983) predicts that all political life will die when freedom of speech and the right to have discussions no longer exist.

The reunification of Vietnam under the leadership of the Vietnamese Communist party put an end to a decade of devastating war in Vietnam. The Vietnamese revolution was indeed the last "Leninist revolution" orchestrated by a single "classic" communist party, and an example of national and social revolution in the countries of the third world (Brocheux and Hemery 1980). Political conflict did not end when the Vietnamese Communist party took control, although most of the opposition leaders went into exile. Vietnamese history may now enter a new era of social change, as other socialist countries have. Social reforms demanded by the people of Eastern European communist countries may indeed in the long term have consequences in "third world" socialist countries such as Vietnam.

Vietnamese immigrants and refugees are people with a long history and awareness of their role in shaping historical processes through political activism. The Parisian Vietnamese community's political activism, which began as early as 1910, is an example of the participation of overseas Vietnamese communities in the shaping of Vietnamese history.

---

5. The driving force and the goal of this system is to change ideologies, consciousness and customs. It is not a learning process which will open people's minds, but rather a process to remodel humankind's whole psychology, people's character, temperament, and ideology. The goal is emotional rather than intellectual in order to create a new mentality, and new behavior.

Chapter 3

Politics among the Vietnamese Immigrants in Paris

Factionalism has been a persistent feature of Vietnamese politics. In France as in Vietnam, conflicting political ideologies deriving from Vietnamese history and identity have divided the Vietnamese immigrant community into competing groups. These factions did not simply emerge from local feuds among leaders in Paris, but rather can be traced to the political conflict that has divided Vietnam for the last sixty years. The fall of Saigon and the reunification of the two Vietnams in 1975 did not end the political conflict in the Parisian Vietnamese community. Instead, the community became even more polarized.

As Duncanson (1968) points out, factionalism in Vietnam was the source of the revolutionary movement as a reaction to the inadequacies of the existing government. Factionalism was seen by Western observers, however, as a fundamental issue for resolving and ending the Indochinese conflict. "The solution to the problems of ordinary people in Vietnam, which they seek through factionalism, does not lie in self-determination at the local government level, for that, on the contrary, has been the initial cause of their trouble" (Duncanson 1968:377). In 1984, I heard a similar argument from a French scholar in Paris when he explained to me that factionalism among Vietnamese immigrants and refugees was only a game and of no political significance. He claimed that French people, in contrast, did have political consciousness. My Vietnamese informants, however, never talked about factions dividing their community. Instead, they talked about political parties based on well-founded ideologies. I argue that Vietnamese factionalism exists in the political discourse of Westerners, whereas the Vietnamese have their own interpretation of politics.

From the late 1950s on, anthropologists were interested in the study of factionalism in small-scale societies (Benedict 1957; Boissevain 1966; Bujra 1973; Nicholas 1965; Siegel and Beals 1960). Nicholas points out that as "conflict groups," factions are political groups that are not corporate and whose members are recruited by leaders. I found, however, that factionalism in the Vietnamese immigrant community does not emerge from a conflict among leaders, but is an extension of the political cleavages in Vietnam. I assert that conflicting ideologies are at the base of Vietnamese factionalism. Dumont (1977:7) defines ideology as "a totality of ideals and values common to a society or to a group of people in general." Although Vietnamese immigrants and refugees share a common value of patriotism, each faction has its own ideal of how the Vietnamese political system should be structured. Cohen (1974) suggests that ideologies are integrative mechanisms for group organization, unifying individual concerns with the goals of the collective. Thus patriotism and conflicting political ideologies can exist side by side. Members of the pro-Hanoi political organization are patriots, but continue to promote division within the community because of their own belief that communism is best for Vietnam. Members of anticommunist organizations are also patriots, but they too engender community division and even go so far as to challenge the legitimacy of the existing government in Vietnam, all in the name of love for their country.

Vietnamese overseas political organizations in France are not technically political parties because they do not compete in electoral politics. Indeed, in France, these organizations belong to a wide political network that encompasses Vietnamese, French, and international political organizations. At different times, and according to the political climate in Vietnam, these organizations have allied with one another to form factions. Today, while the Union Générale des Vietnamiens en France (UGVF) (General Union of Vietnamese in France) supports the Vietnamese Communist party, the anticommunist political organizations, having no support from Vietnamese political parties, have created an overseas political network to oppose the Vietnamese Communist party.

The Vietnamese Political Arena

In the Vietnamese political arena, factionalism is the product of a dynamic process whereby groups seek to gain or maintain power in the Vietnamese community. When and how did the conflict among political organizations emerge in the immigrant community? How do these organizations compete with each other for power and for the support of the immigrants and refugees?

The political activities of Vietnamese immigrants in France between 1910 and 1920 are largely undocumented (Hemery 1975:8). A surprising number of leaders of the Vietnamese Communist party since early in the century have been themselves immigrants to France. Ho Chi Minh stayed in France from 1917 to 1923, and Nguyen An Ninh, an early anticolonial activist, lived for long periods in France and Europe on three occasions between 1919 and 1929.

Between 1918 and 1920, Paris was a magnet that attracted many of those under colonial rule (Hemery 1975:8). Indian and Korean nationalists were involved in political activities generated by the Versailles Conference, which was geared toward the founding of new nations. Hemery suggests that it may have been the explosive climate of Paris at that time that awakened political awareness among members of the Vietnamese immigrant community.

According to Hemery, the first Vietnamese organizations in France were created before World War I. Even though they were mostly nonpolitical, Vietnamese social and cultural activities embodied "nationalist" sentiments, and some had close ties with overtly political groups. Dong Bao Than Ai (L'Amitié Indochinoise) (The Indochinese Friendship), created by Phan Van Truong in 1912, had such links with the underground political organization L'Association des Patriotes Annamites (The Association of the Annamese Patriots), which he cofounded two years later. L'Association des Patriotes was dissolved by the French police in 1915 because of its anticolonial activities in Paris. But it was recreated in 1919 under the name of Groupe des Patriotes Annamites (Group of the Annamese Patriots). Between 1920 and 1922, this was the most active of the immigrant political organizations of the "colonized countries." The organization's membership included many Vietnamese immigrants such as Nguyen An Ninh and Nguyen The Truyen. This group published *Les Revendications du Peuple Annamite*, six thousand copies of which were distributed from 1919 to 1920. Then, with the Madagascar organizations, it created l'Union Intercoloniale (The Intercolonial Union), from which was published *Le Paria* (1922–26). L'Union Intercoloniale, founded in 1901, included members belonging to the indigenous populations of various French colonies, among them Martinique, Guadeloupe, Madagascar, Algeria, Senegal, and Vietnam. According to the French police, by the end of 1923, Nguyen Ai Quoc (later known as Ho Chi Minh) was already actively involved in the leadership of l'Union Intercoloniale (Hemery 1975:11).

Marr argues that the Vietnamese intellectuals overseas took the lead in discussing specific critical political and social developments inside the colony. In Paris, Moscow, and Canton, for example, Vietnamese writers were able to publish materials on Vietnam more freely than the writers in Vietnam itself, and were analyzing "the Bank of Indochina, the conditions of Vietnamese peasants, miners and plantation workers, or causes of high mortality" (Marr 1981:11).

The period between 1920 and 1922 also witnessed the splintering of the Vietnamese community into two separate political factions, a radical and activist one led by Nguyen Ai Quoc and Nguyen The Truyen (both members of the Communist party), and a more moderate one led by Phan Chau Trinh, who encouraged a policy of compromise with the French government.

Both factions shared a similar goal of creating a national state, but they disagreed on the political channels needed to build such a state and on the form it would take. Nguyen Ai Quoc wanted a communist Vietnam based on radical socialist reforms adapted to Vietnamese society and yet integrated into the international communist revolution. In contrast, Phan Chau Trinh was a partisan of slow reform of Vietnam based on educating the Vietnamese people (Hemery 1975:12). Until 1925, the two political factions participated in meetings together. In 1927, conservative nationalists agreed to work with the French toward creating an independent Vietnam. This decision led the radical faction to look elsewhere for allies. They reorganized their group under the name of Viet Nam Doc Lap Dang (VNDLD), also called the Parti Annamite de l'Indépendance (Annamese Party for Independence), and became part of l'Union Intercoloniale allied with the Chinese Kuomintang in 1925 (Hemery 1975:16).

In 1926, a rush of Vietnamese students arrived in France. According to Huynh Kim Khanh (1982:47), "This influx was a result of the reprisals against students and office workers who had been mobilizing for Phan Chau Trinh's funeral." This new generation of Vietnamese had already been exposed to nationalist ideologies back in Vietnam. Huynh Kim Khanh (1982:47), however, argues that Paris and Aix en Provence became

> the external training grounds for the future leadership of the Vietnamese revolutionary activists where they received their initial tools — revolutionary theory, organizational techniques and practical experience to make the revolution in the home country.

Upon their arrival in France, these students affected the then-existing factions and the political institutions of the French Vietnamese community. They added some more elements as well. They not only organized their own political groups within their universities but also participated in existing political organizations. For instance, in 1928 the VNDLD (later known as Vietnamese Communist Party) was reorganized under the leadership of a student group publishing a newspaper called *La Résurrection*. VNDLD participation in the Sixth International Communist Congress led to the creation of the first Vietnamese Communist party.

While the VNDLD was gaining support among students and workers, the conservative nationalist political faction was losing support. In France, Vietnamese students tended to join the more progressive anticolonial Vietnamese political organizations (Hemery 1975). In 1929 the Association Générale des Etudiants Indochinois de Paris (General Association of the Indochinese Students of Paris), which had supported the nationalist conservative faction, collapsed and was replaced by a revolutionary nationalist student group (Hemery 1975:30). Thereafter the Vietnamese community in France was politically well organized. Most political activities were carried out underground and consisted of: (1) organizing an intellectual group to support the Vietnamese revolution and to educate Vietnamese immigrant workers on the political situation in Vietnam and (2) publishing political materials aimed at two different audiences, Vietnamese immigrants in France and revolutionaries back in Vietnam.

Radicalization continued with the emergence of a Vietnamese Trotskyist organization in the Parisian Vietnamese political arena in the mid-1930s. Marr (1981) claims that from 1930 to 1937, the Vietnamese Trotskyists, a handful of Vietnamese students and workers, were willing to demonstrate in Paris side by side with the Vietnamese communists. As a radical political group, the Trotskyists advocated an international proletarian revolution. For their leader, Ta Thu Thau, "the primary threat was an alliance between French capitalism and the native bourgeoisie" (Marr 1981:388). In 1933, some members of the Indochinese Communist party and some Trotskyists published the newspaper *La Lutte* to advance a joint slate of workers' candidates to the Municipal Council. In France, according to my informants, the Trotskyist organization was growing. They actively recruited members among the workers and soldiers. Meanwhile in Vietnam, the conflict between the Indochinese Communist party and the Trotskyists escalated. The Trotskyists condemned Stalin for perverting the Vietnamese revolution and for wanting to build a Soviet empire. In late 1945, the Indochinese Communist party launched a campaign against the Trotskyists in Saigon, and killed most of their leaders. My informant, a seventy-year-old Trotskyist, reports that this action outraged the Trotskyists in Paris, who then felt they could no longer participate with the Vietnamese communists in the revolution. By 1984, the Vietnamese Trotskyist organization in France consisted of a marginal group of individuals who refused to ally themselves with any other group involved in the Vietnamese factional conflict.

In 1939, at the beginning of World War II, twenty thousand Vietnamese workers and eight thousand Vietnamese soldiers arrived in France. Since they had been recruited from rural areas, most of them had little education or political awareness (Le Huu Khoa 1983). After the Germans defeated the French and occupied France, these workers were sent into unoccupied France (the Midi) as a nonfighting branch of the French military. After settling into military camps, these Vietnamese worked in nearby factories and on farms. According to one informant, a sixty-five-year-old

Trotskyist, the Parisian Vietnamese political organizations led by the students immediately made efforts to win the support of these temporary immigrants (Hemery 1975).

The political situation in Vietnam influenced the Vietnamese political arena in France. The Japanese, who had occupied Vietnam, gave their support to the Vietnamese nationalist movement. The VNDLD (or Vietminh) became the recognized force fighting against the French. In 1944 under Japanese patronage, the Vietminh declared the independence of Vietnam and established a new government (Devillers 1952:132).

Back in France the diminished nationalist conservative faction kept a low profile in the Vietnamese community. A Vietnamese Trotskyist told me: "At that time during World War II, the conservatives were not interested in increasing their membership among Vietnamese immigrants, but rather in gaining more power through an alliance with the Germans." In fact, the German government was offering support to nationalist political groups of all colonized countries. Fearing that with German backing the conservative faction would gain the immigrants' support, Vietnamese communist and Trotskyist political groups vigorously campaigned to recruit members from the newly arrived Vietnamese immigrants. A large quantity of political materials was circulated in the military camps, and there was always a communist or Trotskyist in the camps busily recruiting members. Duc's experience illustrates what was going on.

Duc arrived in France in 1942 along with many fellow countrymen. Even though he did not have much education, he knew how to read and write in both Vietnamese and French. He often helped his countrymen read and write letters. Soon he began an evening class to increase their proficiency in the Vietnamese language:

> Up until then I was not very aware of the political activities of the Vietnamese immigrants in France. One day, however, I got into a discussion with a comrade who was also teaching an evening class. He was a communist and he gave me some books to read. Every night we got together and talked about politics. He wanted me to join the Vietnamese communist group, but I just could not do it. I did not totally agree with him on a number of political issues. Later on I was very sick

and spent a month in a military hospital. I met another comrade who gave me a political "tract" from a Trotskyist student group in Paris. The comrade was very kind and he explained to me what the Trotskyist ideology was all about. At that time, I did not understand most of the theoretical jargon, but the overall political idea appealed to me. Back in the camp I started reading more books on Trotsky, and at night I would gather with other comrades to discuss some political issues. After a year, I was spending most of my time writing political propaganda to be sent to other camps. Later I met other comrades from Paris at a Vietnamese congress in Marseille in 1945. Before that I was not very well informed about what was going on in Vietnam.

In 1945, with the war over, most of the Vietnamese workers and military men were sent back to Vietnam, and only about three thousand remained in France. In Vietnam, the situation obviously had also changed radically with the creation of the Republic of Vietnam under the leadership of Ho Chi Minh.

From 1945 to 1965, there was a continual migration of Vietnamese people into France. Their motives for leaving Vietnam were quite different from those of the previous migrants. These migrants fell into two main categories: single men and families. Most of the young men, whose ages ranged from fifteen to twenty-five, came to Europe to pursue their studies in order to avoid the draft in Vietnam (Le Huu Khoa 1983). The families, on the other hand, were Catholic refugees from North Vietnam, most of whom had fled to South Vietnam and later migrated to France. After the withdrawal of French troops from South Vietnam in 1955, those Vietnamese who held French citizenship were able to go to France under the status of "repatriated." The post-1954 Vietnamese migration was a sporadic movement that lasted ten years (Simon 1981). There is no offical census data on the number of Vietnamese who arrived in France between 1955 and 1965. But it has been estimated that the number of people who arrived already holding French citizenship, a number that included individuals of both Vietnamese and French origin, was about thirty thousand to thirty-five thousand (Simon 1981).

The Geneva agreement of 1954 ended French colonial power

in Vietnam and established two Vietnamese states: the Socialist Republic of Vietnam and the (South) Vietnamese Democratic Republic. The subsequent involvement of the United States in Vietnam heightened the conflict within the Vietnamese community in France. Two main political factions emerged: pro-Hanoi and anticommunist (Le Huu Khoa 1983).

In the Vietnamese community, during the Vietnamese war of 1955 to 1975, political activities reached their peak. Intensified activity corresponded with major events of the war: the Tet Offensive in 1968, the negotiations in Paris between 1968 and 1972, the American offensive in the summer of 1972, and the fall of Saigon in 1975. This activity occurred primarily in the intellectual milieu and around universities (Le Huu Khoa 1983:68). At that time the procommunist or pro-Hanoi faction enjoyed great popularity among Vietnamese students. This group used the media to inform the French people about the war and to gain support from the French government. The anticommunist group had difficulty finding any audience until the collapse of South Vietnam sent a new wave of mostly southern refugees to France.

The pro-Hanoi faction's gains in popular support in the Vietnamese community were also due to the French attitude and the French government's policies toward the two Vietnams and American interventionist policy in Vietnam. During the 1960s, under the leadership of Charles de Gaulle, France took a strong stand against American policy in Vietnam. The French government deplored American military escalation in Vietnam, and in particular the bombing policy against Hanoi.

On the other hand, the Vietnamese community's lack of support for the Vietnamese anticommunist organizations was exacerbated by the worsening of diplomatic relations between Paris and Saigon. De Gaulle, who had advocated a neutral regime in South Vietnam, challenged the legitimacy of the leaders of South Vietnam and, after massive numbers of American troops arrived in Vietnam in 1965, considered them American lackeys (Sullivan 1978). Furthermore, the French Vietnamese community itself included over seventy thousand Vietnamese, many of whom were from the south but opposed the Thieu/Ky leadership (Sullivan 1978).

While French-American relations on the issue of Vietnam, as

well as France's relationship with South Vietnam, got worse, in the 1960s there were gradual improvements in the diplomatic relations between Paris and Hanoi in spite of old quarrels between France and the Vietminh. Although the North Vietnamese blamed the French government for facilitating American intervention in Vietnamese affairs after the Geneva Agreement, they were gratified by French public statements against American policy in South Vietnam (Sullivan 1978). From the early 1960s on, there was a regular channel of communication between Hanoi and Paris, although there was no formal ambassadorial representation either in France or in North Vietnam until 1968, when the French government offered Paris as the site for the peace talks.

When I arrived back in Paris in 1984, I found the Vietnamese community still divided into two factions. The political arena had changed demographically, however, with the arrival of so many Vietnamese refugees. The twenty thousand refugees who arrived in France from 1975 to 1982 had fled the communist regime and were much more likely to support the anticommunist faction. The procommunist faction maintained its political power among long-established immigrants and wanted to gain additional support among the refugees. Anticommunist organizations became increasingly active and attempted to turn the new refugees against the procommunists.

Paradoxically, members of the long-established community who were settled and integrated into French society represented an "aristocracy" among Vietnamese immigrants. The refugees were a different breed. They had fled Vietnam and were forced to abandon their property. Upon arrival in France, they found themselves having to take work where they could find it and were painfully aware that they were poor in comparison with those long settled in Paris. This class difference between the factions served to heighten political tensions.

The Political Alliances

French political issues are generally not part of the agenda of Vietnamese political organizations, whose loyalty is obviously to Vietnam. Leaders of these organizations are concerned with French politics, however, if they have an impact on Vietnamese politics.

My informants told me that Parisian Vietnamese political leaders sought alliance with French political parties only over issues directly related to the Vietnamese political arena. French political party leaders, on the other hand, see Vietnamese immigrants and refugees as potential voters, and seek their support through alliances with Vietnamese political organizations.

Current alliances between Vietnamese political organizations and French political parties emerged from a long-standing conflict among these parties over French colonialism. From the beginning of colonial expansion, French political parties have been divided over the colonial issue.

French Colonialism

Although French colonialism began in the early years of the nineteenth century, as Girardet (1972) points out, there was no awareness in French society of colonialism. Neither were there political arguments over this colonial expansion, as was the case later on. The colonial experience was shared by only three groups: (1) the military, who wanted to have strategic access to various parts of the world to safeguard its navy; (2) the French Catholic church, eager to spread the faith, and requesting protection from the French government; and 3) the economist philosophers who saw in colonialism a way to utilize unexploited natural resources, such as lands and raw materials, and to use the labor of indigenous peoples.

Girardet (1972) argues that French colonial expansion under the Third Republic marked the beginning of what he calls "French imperialism." The French nation was no longer seen as limited to its own geographical boundaries, but extended to encompass its conquered territories and their citizens (1972). "C'est là, . . . la véritable colonisation, celle qui apporte à la métropole les richesses si l'on veut, mais surtout la grandeur et la force" (1972:31).[1] In the first years of the Third Republic, colonialism was not a subject of discourse for any specific political parties, but by 1873, the Repub-

---

1. This is indeed the true colonialism, the one which gives the mother country not only wealth but also greatness and strength.

licans at the head of the government started a campaign to promote colonial expansion. In 1880, Prime Minister Jules Ferry,
who was an important political figure in the history of French
colonialism, declared Tunisia a protectorate. Four years later he
claimed French sovereignty over Annam (1972:45). Girardet argues that Ferry's colonial policy rested on three main arguments:
(1) colonialism would allow French industries to control certain
raw materials; (2) Western societies had the duty to help non-
Western societies to reach higher civilization; and (3) France
should compete with other European nations to gain power in the
world through colonial expansion (Girardet 1972).

Colonization became a controversial issue in French politics.
At the beginning of the twentieth century, the first opposition to
French colonial policy was expressed by socialist political writers.
In their articles, the socialists condemned modern colonialism,
which they claimed was the direct consequence of French capitalist
expansion (1972:105). After World War I, the Third Republic
gained the French population's support for its colonial policies by
citing the support of the colonial army in this war, so the socialists
kept a low profile.

In 1920, and then in 1928, the Congress of International
Communism marked a turning point in the history of French political action against colonialism. The Congress decided to integrate colonized peoples into its struggle for the international
proletariat (Girardet 1972:139). From 1930 onwards, the French
communist newspaper *L'Humanité*, in support of anticolonialist indigenous political organizations, published reports on the social
and political conditions of those colonies opposed to French
colonialism. The first Vietnamese political organizations in
France focused on anticolonialist issues. In 1927, the VNDLD
won support from the French Communist party, and has maintained that alliance ever since.

Vietnamese Alliance with French Parties

At that time, the French Communist party (Parti Communiste
Français [PCF]), was the only European political force to support
Vietnamese independence (Hemery 1975). The PCF became the
link between the Communist International and the Vietnamese

Revolutionary parties. *L'Humanité* (April 5, 1928) summarized the PCF's goal as follows:

> "Le peuple indochinois . . . sait que la seule solution à sa tragique situation est dans l'indépendance totale de son pays . . . Mais cette indépendance ne s'obtiendra que . . . s'il sait unifier ses forces dans un parti national orienté nettement vers la lutte implacable pour l'indépendance. (Hemery 1975:37)[2]

In 1928 two Vietnamese leaders of the VNDLD joined the French Communist party to participate in the Sixth International Congress. This action resulted in the creation of the first Vietnamese communist cell within the French Communist party. In 1929, the French communists promptly initiated a political campaign for Vietnamese independence. They focused on the Vietnamese immigrant community in France, recruiting members among workers and students and training the Vietnamese in communist strategies. From then on, *L'Humanité* regularly published an Indochinese section written by young Vietnamese communists. The PCF also sponsored the writing of underground political propaganda materials in the Vietnamese language called *quoc-ngu* (Hemery 1975).

From 1946 to 1954, after the country was divided into two Vietnams, the VNDLD gave strong backing to the government of Hanoi. With the PCF, the leaders of the VNDLD branch in France condemned American intervention in Vietnam, and the two groups worked together to gain the support of the French people.

During the 1960s, with the escalation of American involvement, there was general disapproval in France toward the American interventionist policy in Vietnam. Sullivan (1978:75) states:

> In France, public distaste for the war was inspired by concern for the human suffering it caused among people for whom the

---

2. The Indochinese people . . . know that the only solution to their tragic situation is the complete independence of their country . . . But this independence will be obtained only . . . if the people unify their forces into a national party clearly oriented toward the implacable struggle for independence.

French felt some affection; consequently, French public opinion objected most violently to American bombing of North Vietnam.

Among the right-wing French political parties, the extreme right, which included both strong French nationalists and pro-Americans, favored the war and avoided criticizing American policy, while the Gaullists openly critized the American policy and the escalation of the war (Sullivan 1978). The French Left, on the other hand, was strongly opposed to the conflict in Vietnam. Although in the early 1960s there was disagreement among the different leftist political parties, such as between the PCF and the French Socialist Party (Le Parti Socialiste Français [PSF]), in the way they should oppose the war, by 1971 they had formed an alliance to stage antiwar demonstrations and forums (Sullivan 1978).

The radical political change in Vietnam in 1975 had a profound impact on political alliances in France. The newly arrived Vietnamese immigrants were of a different breed. As refugees from a communist regime, and with no prospect of returning to Vietnam in the near future, these people have accepted their resettlement in France as a temporary situation, but realize that it may be for a long time. As they often told me, "We will wait as long as it takes to free Vietnam and one day we will be able to return." The Vietnamese emigrating to France between World War I and World War II had always seen themselves as temporary immigrants also. Ironically, these long-established Vietnamese settlers, who had supported the Hanoi government and planned to return to Vietnam, realized after 1975 that there was no place for them in the new Vietnamese society (see chap. 4). Consequently, many of these Vietnamese became French citizens.

French politicians in search of new party members started competing vigorously to recruit the new refugees. They bargained with Vietnamese leaders for votes in exchange for political support. Anti-communists used their allies' political strength to pressure the government not to have any relationship with Hanoi, while pro-Hanoi political groups pushed their allies to facilitate communication with Hanoi (see chaps. 5 and 6).

French politicians also competed to recruit refugees who had not yet joined any Vietnamese political organization. In 1984, the mayor of Paris, Jacques Chirac, representing the Right, competed with François Mitterrand's Socialist party for the allegiance of these refugees. After his party's electoral victory in 1981, Mitterrand could offer government programs for social services to the refugees. In addition, the Socialist party sponsored numerous social and cultural events proposed by the UGVF. Vietnamese artists were invited to perform in France to promote social and economic exchange between France and Vietnam. Chirac rose to the occasion by offering city buildings to anticommunist groups for their social activities. In the thirteenth arrondissement of Paris, where most of the Asian population has settled, anticommunist organizations were granted recreational facilities. As one of my informants, a twenty-two-year-old Vietnamese student, explained, "The mayor is providing us with a lot of support in the hope that we will mobilize our group to break the power of the Communist party in the thirteenth."

Vietnamese Political Organizations

Vietnamese organizations are of two types: legal and underground. Legal organizations have legal standing under French legislation, while underground organizations operate illegally. Whether legal or not, all these organizations are called "associations," the term referring to "a gathering of people sharing a common interest" (*Dictionnaire Larousse* 1971).

Each faction is composed of a number of social groups that acquire legal recognition as associations. According to French law, an association is a nonprofit organization governed by the law of 1910. Its regulations are explicitly stated in its application for recognition. In order to gain the status of an "association," a group has to apply at the "préfecture de police," police headquarters, and if accepted, the new association is announced in the "Journal Officiel," the official journal. As a recognized social group, an association has: (1) its own headquarters; (2) access to a public place to organize social and cultural events; (3) the right to hold meetings; and (4) the right to recruit members. The formal structure of an association is defined as a democratic body with a president, vice-presidents, secretaries, and treasurers.

An association is prohibited from conducting political activities. This restriction, however, is not included in the application regulations. When I asked a French official to explain this omission, he replied that when he receives an application, he informs the members of a future association that an association is a social and cultural group and must have no political purposes. Afterward he admitted that this law is not enforced.

Vietnamese associations do not fit the French legal definition because their activities are more political than social. Various associations are linked to Vietnamese political organizations. Contrary to French law, these associations are directly involved in Vietnamese politics. While looking through a number of Vietnamese association applications, I came across a 1954 application that explicitly stated its political goals. The association intended to establish a political network to support the Democratic party in South Vietnam. On another occasion I attempted to examine the application of an anticommunist association, but was told that the government had dissolved the association because of its political activities. Its file was thus inaccessible to the public. In both cases, French officials refused to explain this obvious inconsistency. The point here is that politics and the enforcement of rules are inextricably related. The law is selectively enforced according to whichever French political party is in power.

Vietnamese associations are by no means independent of the French political scene, because the French political climate is very influential. This fact is illustrated by the change in the French government's treatment of Vietnamese associations after Vietnam achieved independence. Until 1954, the French authorities were very concerned with Vietnamese associations in France because of their anticolonial political activities. Underground political associations were thus subjected to police harassment. Student and worker associations were suspected of alliances with Vietnamese political organizations, and were kept under close surveillance.

According to my informants, the immigrants were strongly nationalist, and wanted to preserve their cultural identity and support their fellow citizens living in Vietnam. Thus they planned to aid the fight for the independence of Vietnam and formed organizations with political as well as social and cultural goals. Their indirect participation in the Vietnamese revolution became the subject of increasing concern for the French government, which saw it as a threat to its colonial authority in Indochina.

Until 1923, the French government had created only a small agency to oversee the activities of the Vietnamese community. In 1923, however, a special office was established, named La Service de Contrôle et d'Assistance des Indigènes des Colonies (CAI) (Office of Control and Assistance for the Indigenous People in the Colonies). The agency became more and more specialized as Vietnamese political activism increased. By 1941 a new bureau, Service Colonial du Contrôle des Indigènes (SCCI) (Office of Control of the Indigenous People), was created to curtail the political activities of these immigrant organizations. Its main role was to serve as a "liaison" office with the Indochinese colonial governor in order to coordinate efforts to track down troublemakers (Archives Nationales de France, Section Outre-Mer, 1929). A great deal of information was exchanged about individuals engaged in (suspicious) political activities.

The French government was primarily concerned with the high incidence of student involvement in political organizations. For instance, on the occasion of the reorganization of a "foyer" (center) for the Indochinese students in Paris, Mr. Fontain, a French authority, stated:

> Toute propagande, toute activité politique sera strictement absolument interdite a l'intérieur du foyer, specialement celle qui mettrait en cause la souveraineté de la France en Indochine . . . Cet article sera appuyé de sanctions sévères.[3]

In the report he submitted to the French government, he added that it was important for the Vietnamese students to feel that they were free and that the government trusted them (Archives Nationales de France, Section Outre-Mer, 1929).

The French government hired a number of Vietnamese "agents" to infiltrate associations as well as political organizations.

---

3. All propaganda, all political activities, especially those which would threaten the sovereignty of France in Indochina will be absolutely forbidden inside the hostel . . . This legislation will be enforced by severe sanctions.

These agents followed the activities of suspicious Vietnamese immigrants and gave reports on all political meetings. In one such report an agent recounted that at one meeting, a Mr. Ho stated that

> a number of Vietnamese Communists went to Spain to join the Spanish political group Frente Popular in order to fight against fascism but that the Vietnamese community in Marseille did not seem yet to be affected by these events. (Archives Nationales de France, Section Outre-Mer, 1937)

In another report of agent "H" (the name was not revealed in the document):

> Sergeant Thiep read newspapers and political propaganda in quoc ngu [the Vietnamese language], published in France, at Le Luat bookstore. It seems that we should consider this man a nationalist. He does not take any publications out of the bookstores and is very cautious at the military camp. (Archives Nationales de France, Section Outre-Mer, 1929)

After Vietnamese independence in 1954, the French attitude toward Vietnamese political activism changed. According to Direr (1982), the year 1965 marked the intensification of American intervention in South Vietnam. It was also a period when the French government believed that the Americans would be successful in Vietnam, and stopped giving its support to the (North) Vietnamese Socialist Republic. In support of the South Vietnamese government, the French government recognized all associations allied with the Democratic party in Vietnam. This official sanction did not extend to the pro-Hanoi political organizations. The French even went so far as to give the South Vietnamese government information on the political activities of "communist organizations." As a member of the UGVF recalled, "During those years we felt threatened by the French police because we knew that they would report any information they could gather on us to the South Vietnamese government."

In 1973, the American government started to pull out its troops from Vietnam, while the French government signed the Accord de Paris with the Vietnamese Socialist Republic. In 1974, the Comité National proclaimed "une politique française au Vietnam" (a French policy in Vietnam) (Direr 1982:15). Two years after the 1975 fall of Saigon, Vietnamese Prime Minister Pham Van Dong made an official visit to Paris, in the springtime. By 1979, the French and Vietnamese governments had established a plan of "coopération" between the two countries.

At present, France is one of the few noncommunist countries with a Vietnamese consulate. The pro-Hanoi association (UGVF) was designated the official representative of the Vietnamese immigrant community in 1978. In 1981 the new French socialist government officially recognized the UGVF as a legal association.

After the anticommunist organization lost their official status, their political activities went underground. The French government maintains an ambiguous stance toward them, because its policy of courting whatever Vietnamese government is currently in power prevents it from openly supporting these organizations. Yet the French continue to grant a great number of Vietnamese newcomers the status of political refugees.

Today the pro-Hanoi faction officially consists of only one association, UGVF. It is a very well structured organization with headquarters in Paris. Considered a communist organization by the French government, the association was forced to carry out its political activities underground for many years. Since the election of the French Socialist party in 1981, the association has been officially recognized. A number of other associations, such as Organisme de Formation Professionnelle et d'Enseignement de Langues (FORMASIE) (Organization of Professional Training and Teaching of Languages) and Loisirs Vacances Franco-Asiatiques (LOVAFRAS) (Asian-French Entertainment and Vacations), which claim to be cultural and social associations, are in fact political allies of the UGVF.

In contrast, approximately one hundred anticommunist associations exist. These associations fall into three categories: (1) social and cultural associations such as L'Alliance Vietnamienne (The Vietnamese Alliance), Hanh Dong (L'Organisation d'Entre-Aide des Refugiés) (Organization of Mutual Assistance for the Refugees), Le Village Vietnamien (The Vietnamese Village), and

L'Assocation d'Entre-Aide des Vietnamiens Agés d'Outre-Mer (Mutual Association for the Overseas Vietnamese Elderly). These primarily organize social and cultural activities, but they also give political support to the anticommunists. (2) Student associations such as L'Association Générale des Etudiants Vietnamiens de Paris (The Association of the Vietnamese Students of Paris) and L'Amicale des Vietnamiens de la Région de Paris-Sud (The Friendship Association of the Vietnamese of South Paris) concentrate on recruitment and fund-raising through cultural and social events. Most members are students or former students. (3) Leadership associations such as the Conseil Mondial des Communautés Vietnamiennes (International Council of Vietnamese Communities) and l'Union des Vietnamiens Libres d'Outre-Mer (The Association of the Free Overseas Vietnamese), formed by former South Vietnamese elites, are the core of the anticommunist faction. Their goal is to prepare a new government to take over when the present Hanoi government is overthrown.

Both the communist and anticommunist factions are supported by religious associations primarily affiliated with Vietnamese religious institutions such as the Catholic church or Buddhist temples. Some temples have openly stated their political alliance with a faction. They may even participate in political activities such as demonstrations or the publishing of political materials. For instance, Buddhists at the "Khanh Anh" temple in Bagneux, a southern suburb of Paris, are well known in the Vietnamese community for their anticommunist activism. The Truc Lam Buddhist temple in Villebon on the outskirts of Paris, built by members of the UGVF, supports the pro-Hanoi faction.

Underground organizations also exist that lack any official status with the French government, but exert great influence within the Vietnamese community. Some have been disbanded by French authorities for carrying out underground political activities, yet they are surprisingly resilient. In 1984, I contacted members of an underground anticommunist association that is involved in assisting military guerrillas in Vietnam. It receives support from anticommunist associations. Although anticommunist leaders consider the organization "radical," they still think it performs a necessary function.

Leadership

The leadership of Vietnamese political organizations is mostly made up of a core of intellectuals. I use the term *intellectuals* as a social category. Aron (1968:290) defines an intellectual as "écrivain ou artiste, l'intellectuel est l'homme des idées; savant ou ingénieur, l'hômme de science."[4] At different times and places the intellectuals have been referred to as "lettrés" (men of letters), "philosophers," "mandarins," "the scholar-gentry" and the intelligentsia (Marr 1981; Aron 1968). In Europe the role of intellectuals in politics, however, emerged only in the late nineteenth century. Aron (1968) suggests that intellectuals started to participate in politics when they questioned the authority of the governments in power. They then took a stand on political issues such as colonialism and capitalism, and analyzed societies.

As discussed earlier in this chapter, many Vietnamese students were sent to Paris to pursue their studies as early as 1926. After graduating from French universities, some of them returned to Vietnam, while others stayed on in France. According to my informants, they did not always choose to stay in France. For instance, World War II prevented many of them from returning to Vietnam. The fall of Saigon in 1975 prevented South Vietnamese students from returning. Even though they were already politicized in Vietnam, these students became even more inclined to pursue politics in the politicized French universities.

Historians disagree on the role Vietnamese intellectuals in France played in the Vietnamese revolution. Woodside (1976) suggests that the Vietnamese overseas student movement of the colonial period did not have any national strategy. He argues that these children of rich families were sent to France to acquire degrees for the sake of individual and family advancement. He points out that while more nationalistic motivations did come into play after 1954, the students from South Vietnam were still from the upper class. In contrast, Marr (1981:11) contends that

---

4. writer, or artist, the intellectual is a man of ideas; scholar or engineer, he is a man of science.

Vietnamese intellectuals overseas took the lead in discussing specific political and social developments inside the colony . . . Ho Chi Minh was the most notable example, but he was followed by scores of other Vietnamese residing for one period of time or another in France, the Soviet Union, and China.

I agree with Woodside that no Vietnamese student movements in France organized as revolutionary political groups. Indeed, political organizations included not only students, but also workers and soldiers. Students, however, took over the leadership of these groups and made significant contributions to the revolution. As Marr (1981) points out, they were able to publish anticolonialist materials on the sociopolitical situation of Vietnam and then smuggled them into Vietnam. Marr (1981) reports that during the 1920s, Vietnamese students in France obtained a broad range of information on the Soviet Union, which led to Ho Chi Minh's visit to Moscow in 1923. He also points out that by 1920 only a few Vietnamese were able to study Marxist-Leninist doctrine in Paris. But by 1929, the "ABC's of Communism" translated into *quoc ngu* was clandestinely distributed, and small study groups were secretly organized by overseas Vietnamese students returning to Vietnam.

Parisian Vietnamese political organizations have also acted as support groups, from which important Vietnamese political figures have emerged. Ho Chi Minh's stay in France without question had a significant impact on the Vietnamese revolution. While living in Paris, Ho Chi Minh gathered around him a number of other Vietnamese revolutionaries. Lacouture (1968) suggests that it was in Paris that Ho Chi Minh served out his apprenticeship in life, politics, and revolution by enduring extreme poverty and sharing the hardships of others. Lacouture (1968) also reports:

Ho Chi Minh played a full part in the Socialist Congress at Tours and joined the Communist group headed by Cachin and Frossard; he published his violent pamphlet "Le Procès de la Colonisation Française"; he set up the Intercolonial Union, becoming founder, editor and distributor of its organ, "Le Paria."

Another example is Ngo Dinh Nhu, Diem's brother, who pursued his prewar studies at the Ecole des Chartes, and who came in contact with Mounier. Impressed by Mounier's ideas, when he returned to Vietnam, Nhu convinced his brother Diem to adopt the philosophy of personalism.

In 1984, I found that most leaders of the Vietnamese political organizations are no longer students but rather, by now, well-established intellectuals and professionals. As former students in France, they had participated in Vietnamese political activities. Students are still involved in these organizations, but they are now considered to be an apprenticeship group that is being trained for future leadership of the Parisian Vietnamese community.

Leaders promote the specific ideologies of their group. Their political discourse always focuses on Vietnam rather than on the personal attributes of the respective leaders. Pro-Hanoi leaders mobilize their followers around the concept of socialism in Vietnam. Anticommunist leaders criticize communist totalitarianism and advocate the creation of a democratic nation in Vietnam.

Issues around Which the Factions Mobilized Vietnamese Immigrants and Refugees in France

The cleavage between the two Vietnamese factions is permanent. This split is perpetuated by the fact that the Vietnamese political organizations have polarized the Parisian Vietnamese immigrants around issues rather than leaders. The mobilizing issues are carefully selected by these political organizations, whose leaders formulate issues in terms designed to appeal to the immigrants in order to gain their support.

In the early 1900s, all Vietnamese political groups shared a common ideology: the creation of a national state to free Vietnam from colonialism. The leaders of the Vietnamese community mobilized the immigrants around social and cultural issues. They emphasized "national pride" and cultural identity, and their goal was to unify these immigrants in order to fight for the independence of their own country.

After the split of the nationalist groups into two separate parties, one led by Ho Chi Minh and the other by Phan Chau Trinh, the issues were couched in terms of political ideology. Under the communist banner, Ho proposed a well-structured organization to fight French colonialism. In his appeal to his fellow immigrants, Ho described Vietnam as an oppressed nation, exploited by French imperialists. He emphasized the need for the Vietnamese to join international alliances. These propaganda materials were well received by the Vietnamese immigrants. Not only had they experienced colonialism directly in Vietnam, but even in France they still suffered from racial discrimination.

French treatment of Vietnamese immigrants in France during World War II was abominable. Duc recalled his experiences in a French military camp in 1942:

> Most of the young Vietnamese men wanted to go back to Vietnam and they did not understand why they had to stay in France when in fact the French were defeated by the Germans, and the French army did not have any role to play. Living conditions were very bad for us. We did not have enough to eat, and did not have enough clothes to protect us against the cold. Since I had a higher status as a translator, I was invited to share meals with the French officers. I went there only once because I was disgusted with the wide array of food they ate while the Vietnamese were starving. Working conditions were not any better. Some of us had to work at the "Salins," a salt factory. I will never forget a young Vietnamese man who lost his foot from walking on the salt all day with no shoes for protection. When I first read materials on the oppression of the Vietnamese people by the French I felt empowered. I realized that we did not have to live like animals with no control over our own life. My comrades and I felt these groups would save us from our misery and allow us to be free men again.

This account of the Vietnamese immigrants in France at that time demonstrates the effectiveness of targeted political issues in mobilizing community support. The communists and the Trotskyists found a sympathetic ear with the immigrants. The nationalist conservatives, however, found little support for their position that there should be a compromise over the independence of Vietnam.

After the 1954 Geneva agreement, Vietnam gained its independence. But the division of the country into two zones brought a new conflict to the French Vietnamese political domain. The issues were no longer focused on the independence of Vietnam, but on the subsequent war.

The pro-Hanoi group was able to gain great support among the immigrants, particularly among students, intellectuals, and the long-established community already supporting Hanoi. They chose the popular issue of the antiwar movement, which was already gaining international support. The call to end the war and withdraw American troops was the political slogan that helped recruit thousands of new members. Long, a forty-five-year-old engineer, described the era:

> During that time I really felt a sense of community. Most of us [students] were activists and believed that with the withdrawal of the American troops in Vietnam that war would end. We spent most of our free time working at the UGVF, going to meetings, putting up signs on the walls of Paris, and going from door to door to inform the French people about the political situation in Vietnam. It was a very exciting time. We spent most of our time together with little concern over our position in the French community because we believed that we would return to Vietnam after the end of the war.

While the pro-Hanoi group mobilized most of the Vietnamese students in France, the groups who supported the South Vietnamese government were not popular around campuses. Tuyen remembered the fights they had had with pro-Hanoi students on the campus of Orsay. He said "They were greater in numbers and had the support of the French. As a minority it was difficult for us to recruit among the Vietnamese students. We did not seem to speak their language." These groups also focused on issues of peace, but they did not believe that the withdrawal of American troops would end the war. They pushed for the status quo of the two Vietnams, and for improvements in the South Vietnamese government.

The last distinctive period is post-1975. With the arrival of thousands of refugees escaping the communist regime, the political balance in the Vietnamese community shifted. The pro-Hanoi group altered the focus of its political appeal. The war was over, but most Vietnamese immigrants who had planned to return to Vietnam could not go back (see chaps. 4 and 5). The UGVF suggested creating a Vietnamese community in France that would support the regime in Hanoi. In order to maintain its power in the long-established community, this group presented Vietnam as a Third World country that needed the support of the Vietnamese communities living abroad. To gain the support of the newly arrived Vietnamese people, UGVF focused on social and cultural issues and tried to remain politically neutral (see chap. 6).

After the fall of Saigon the pro-South Vietnamese faction focused on anticommunism. This group easily found support from the newly arrived Vietnamese community. They warned the refugees that the UGVF was politically allied with the communists. In all their social events, the anticommunist group made statements against communism and against participating in any social and cultural events organized by the UGVF. They recruited members to establish a Vietnamese government-in-exile ready to replace Hanoi at the first opportunity.

Chapter 4

Vietnamese Immigrants and Refugees as an Ethnic Minority in France

The Vietnamese, along with the Laotians, Cambodians, and Southeast Asian Chinese, form the new Asian ethnic minorities in France (Simon-Barouh 1982).[1] Barth (1969) and Leach (1954) have argued that ethnicity, as a marker of a distinct identity (either self-ascribed or ascribed by others), is based on social interactions defined by a set of roles and statuses. I define the boundaries of Vietnamese ethnic identity as deriving principally from a set of social behaviors and relations woven into a social hierarchy that is itself derived from Confucian doctrine.

As Cohen (1969) demonstrates in the case of Africa, this ethnic distinctiveness or "retribalization" is a process whereby ethnic groups mobilize to gain political power in a highly competitive urban environment. These scholars put forward the argument that an ethnic group becomes politicized when it becomes self-conscious of its cultural and social distinctiveness.

As documented in the previous chapters, Vietnamese immigrants and refugees in France have remained highly politicized around issues related to their homeland. But unlike other French ethnic minorities, like the Corsicans, Bretons, Basques, and Alsatians, the Asian ethnic minorities do not form a political interest group since they do not try to compete for political power in France. Simon-Barouh (1982) argues that Asian immigrants iden-

---

1. This new Asian population in France is estimated at 150,000 to 200,000 (Simon-Barouh 1982:62).

tify themselves as Vietnamese, Laotians, or Cambodians rather than as members of a single Asian ethnic minority (this is less true of the generation born in France). Furthermore, the French government identifies Asians collectively as foreigners (despite the fact that most are French citizens), whose political activities, unlike those of French ethnic minorities, are not perceived as a threat to French national security. Asian political activities focus on internal national issues of their respective homelands, rather than on those of France.

These facts suggest that politicization among Vietnamese immigrants and refugees is an expression of their preexisting cultural identity, rather than an assertion of their ethnicity in the French political arena. Like language, religion, and customs, Vietnamese politics in France is a cultural trait that Vietnamese immigrants and refugees brought with them and that they maintain in France.

Immigrants in France

Today, it is estimated that eleven million French citizens are descendants of recent immigrants (*Le Monde,* October 1984), but unlike Americans, the French have not integrated the tradition of immigration into their culture. They do not see themselves as a nation descended from immigrants. In the mid-nineteenth century, large-scale immigration began with the arrival of white immigrant laborers, consisting mostly of Belgians and Italians, who were absorbed into mainstream French society after a generation (Noirel 1984).

French decolonization attracted a new kind of immigrant, less easily absorbed. These immigrants were increasingly nonwhite, Muslim rather than Christian, and regarded as inferior by the French. In the late 1970s and early 1980s, high unemployment rates have exacerbated racial conflict between the French and the nonwhite immigrants, especially Arabs.

Today, the conflict over immigration remains highly politicized. The French leftist Socialist and Communist parties side with the immigrants in order to gain support from those who can become French citizens, while the French party of the extreme Right, "Le Front National," uses the problem of immigration as a platform in order to regain power in the next election. An incident of racial conflict became a political issue in January 1984. Renault, a factory on the northern outskirts of Paris employing predominantly nonwhite immigrants, wanted to fire half of its workers because of a slowdown in production. The union, a leftist organization, opposed this policy and launched a major strike. After a month of negotiation, tensions rose between immigrant strikers and nonstriking French workers, and the factory became the battleground of racial violence between the two groups.

The French government has historically taken great pains to track the movement of both foreigners and natives within its territory (DeLey 1983). In 1932, the first French law limiting immigration established quotas for foreigners with work identification cards. During the postwar period of 1945, an active immigration policy was formulated to provide the additional manpower necessary to reconstruct the economy and to increase the population growth rate (Kennedy-Brenner 1979). The French government created a National Office of Immigration and modified its immigration law to institute three types of residence permits: a temporary permit (valid for one year), an ordinary permit (three years), and a privileged permit (ten years). The new law permitted the expulsion of foreigners who allegedly constituted a "threat to public order or to the public credit" (DeLey 1983:198–99). Through the Ministry of Foreign Affairs, successive governments have negotiated a number of manpower agreements (Kennedy-Brenner 1979).[2] By 1960, the government lost control of immigration. Illegal immigration, particularly of North Africans, increased during the succeeding decade.[3] By 1973, the period of economic expansion in France had ended. In July 1974, the French government announced a provisional halt to the further entry of immigrant workers (Kennedy-Brenner 1979). Yet despite government anti-immigration policies between 1974 and 1981, the

---

2. Bilateral legal manpower agreements were concluded successively with Greece (1954), Spain (1961), Morocco, Tunisia, Portugal (1963), Algeria (1964), and Yugoslavia and Turkey (1965). Nationals of former African colonies south of the Sahara were initially allowed to enter France without obtaining a work or residence permit.

3. In 1969 a report was presented to the Economic Social Council stressing the need for a "real immigration policy." This report pointed out the current policy's incompatibility with manpower needs, the growing unemployment of foreigners, housing shortages, lack of adequate health-care facilities, and the difficulties immigrants experience in assimilation (Kennedy-Brenner 1979:27).

number of foreigners residing in France (especially illegal aliens) did not decrease (1983:201). In recent years, France has experienced a dramatic increase in the number of Chinese who enter France illegally.

Immigration has become a hot political issue in France. Mr. Le Pen, leader of "le Front National," a right-wing political organization, has made restricted immigration an important part of his platform. He advocates the return of all "temporary immigrants" to their own countries as a way of reducing unemployment in France and restoring French unity. He claims that cultural differences between the French and immigrants make assimilation impossible.

Over the past two years, Le Pen's political party has achieved national renown. His campaign has a wide appeal among members of all strata of French society. This politician's popularity can be attributed to two factors. The first is his blatant racism, with which many French are in silent agreement. Marcilly (1984:201) reports, "Le Pen dit tout haut, ce que tout le monde pense tout bas."[4] The second factor is his well-planned campaign, which has been highly publicized by the media. So far his political campaign has focused primarily on North African immigrants. Even though the growing Asian population is becoming a more and more "visible community," it has not yet become the major target of his political crusade.

French attitudes toward the Vietnamese are quite different from those they express toward Arabs and blacks. The Vietnamese community is so far considered nonpolitical and trouble free by most French, who stereotype Vietnamese immigrants and refugees as hard-working and quiet. According to my Vietnamese informants, French racism toward the Vietnamese is more subtle and latent than that toward most other ethnic minorities. For instance, a number of Parisians with whom I talked, and who knew I was doing fieldwork in the Vietnamese community, complained that there were too many Vietnamese in France and that they were already taking over the thirteenth arrondissement. The French, however, do not differentiate the Vietnamese from the Chinese. This Parisian neighborhood, for instance, is not Vietnamese but

---

4. Le Pen expresses openly what everyone else is thinking to themselves.

rather is populated by ethnic Chinese from Southeast Asia and from Hong Kong. The French popular concept of the "péril jaune" (yellow peril), which connotes the fear of being controlled by Asians, and which was once attributed to China with its over-population, is now being used by French people in reference to Asian migration to France. One day I had a discussion with the owner of a computer software company who told me that he had had some bad experiences with his Vietnamese employees. He said that even though they were hard workers and extremely qualified in the field of computer science, they were difficult to get along with. He explained that they did not get along well or share valuable information with other employees, nor did they in his view accept criticism constructively. He said that in the future, he would hire a less qualified French engineer over a Vietnamese person because he believed that the quality of the service his business provided required good relations among employees. This example is of course an isolated case, but it does reflect this "latent racism." Although the French have shown compassion toward Vietnamese refugees, they are not yet ready to accept and deal with cultural diversities in their own work environment. Many Vietnamese students regard computer science studies as a field with future employment possibilities in France, and yet some of my Vietnamese informants have expressed concern about "a field where there will be too many Vietnamese." This comment reflects the Vietnamese understanding of French attitudes toward Asians and other ethnic groups in France. The Vietnamese fear that if they are too concentrated in a specific sector of the French economy, they might be viewed as a threat, and could provoke the French to be resentful of them.

Before 1954, the French Vietnamese community was composed of voluntary immigrants. The withdrawal of French troops from Indochina in 1955 and the fall of Saigon in 1975, however, prompted a huge influx of Vietnamese refugees to France. The refugee status of post-1954 Vietnamese immigrants was never questioned by the French or by the Vietnamese. By contrast, the refugee status of the second post-war wave of Vietnamese immigrants has been the subject of political concern.

In his study of the French Vietnamese immigrants, Le Huu Khoa (1983) argues that the Vietnamese immigrants leaving Vietnam after 1975 did not flee due to political persecution but rather for economic reasons. He states:

> Le problème de l'exode des réfugiés n'a pas été formulé dans sa vraie dimension économique: ils fuient le sous-développement; le début de l'exil correspond à la fin de l'inévitable inadaptation à l'émergence d'une nouvelle organisation sociale. (Le Huu Khoa 1983:94)[5]

Khoa suggests here that the "refugee category" does not properly apply to the Vietnamese immigrant, but has been used by the media for political propaganda. However, because Khoa is a member of the UGVF and his theory fits the organization's political discourse, some might discount it.

The French socialist government's policies toward the refugees from Vietnam are complex because of its earlier diplomatic relations with Hanoi. After the fall of Saigon, the government restricted asylum to Vietnamese who: (1) had worked for French businesses or the French government in Vietnam; (2) were French citizens; (3) had relatives in France; (4) were picked up at sea by French ships; or (5) were selected in refugee camps of Southeast Asia. In 1979, the Vietnamese government agreed with the French and the British to give exit visas to all those who wished to leave to join their families, except for prisoners, those considered to possess state secrets, and those who were in the military (Wilson 1983:11). Every week since then, an Air France plane carrying Vietnamese people has arrived in Paris from Ho Chi Minh City. In 1984, I was told by my informants that about 200 Vietnamese were arriving weekly from Vietnam. Upon arrival these newcomers are held in a refugee relocation center for two weeks. There they are instructed by French authorities to declare themselves "refugees." This policy is controversial in the Vietnamese communities. Members of the UGVF claim that many newcomers are not refugees and should not be treated as such. Some go to France to

---

5. The problem of the refugees' departure has not been studied in terms of its actual economic dimension. The refugees are escaping an under-developed country. The beginning of these people's exile corresponds with the end of the inevitable tumult caused by the emergence of a new social system.

visit relatives, while others are immigrants who want to be re-united with their families.

On the other hand, anticommunist leaders claim that the UGVF members are lying and are using the "family reunification program" to get their own families out of Vietnam. As Manh, a thirty-year-old leader of an anticommunist organization, comments, "All Vietnamese people leaving Vietnam today are political refugees." He blames the Vietnamese communist government for the bad economic situation and believes that people fled for fear of repression and of losing their livelihoods.

The other argument is that France has closed its borders to immigration, and therefore can admit Vietnamese only as refugees. This policy has been kept a secret from the public and the media. An immigration official told me that any information on the nature of the Hanoi-Paris agreement could not be given out without the approval of the French government. He added, "In the past, information on the number of Vietnamese refugees in France was published in local newspapers. The government of Hanoi was extremely upset and threatened to discontinue diplomatic relations with Paris." Considering that the French government has restricted migration laws for the last few years, I conclude that the publication of this information would outrage immigrants and refugees from other parts of the world, especially those from Africa.

The lack of studies on ethnic minority participation in French politics is another indicator of the marginalization of immigrant groups in France. This situation contrasts markedly with that of ethnic minorities in the United States. In the United States, immigrant groups have generally responded to prevailing social conditions by becoming self-conscious ethnic minorities. They have integrated into the pluralist American society as "special interest groups" and thus participate in local politics. Nowadays, Jews, Chinese, Chicanos, and Japanese, for example, have a recognized political clout and are thus courted by American politicians. This kind of pluralism, however, is absent in France, where the concept of a pluralist society is only a recent phenomenon (Gallissot 1984).

The lack of political participation among immigrants in their host country is also observed in other European countries. In his study on the political participation of ethnic minorities in the

Netherlands, Rath (1983) points out that the Moluccans, Surinamers, and Antillians do not form political interest groups and therefore have limited influence in Dutch politics. He suggests that this is partly due to the fact that many immigrants are not Dutch citizens and therefore do not have the right to vote. He notes also that these immigrants' lack of knowledge of the Dutch political system and their focus only on the politics of their homeland have prevented them from using the political channels in the Netherlands.

The situation of the ethnic minorities in the Netherlands is similar to that of the Vietnamese in France and yet significantly different. While most Vietnamese immigrants and refugees are French citizens today, they rarely participate in French politics. I argue, however, that the naturalization of Vietnamese immigrants and refugees cannot be used as an indicator of their political integration in French politics. Portes and Mozo (1985), for instance, compare the citizenship and voting patterns of both Cuban refugees and Mexican immigrants in the United States. They suggest that:

> The rate at which an immigrant group acquires citizenship is important, first, as an indicator of its collective desire to become integrated in the host society and, second, as a measure of its potential political power through electoral participation. (Portes and Mozo 1985:39)

Portes and Mozo (1985) conclude that, unlike any other immigrant groups in the United States, Cubans have a large turnout in local elections, voting for conservative parties who are strongly opposed to the current Cuban government. Like the Cubans, the Vietnamese have a high rate of naturalization, but very few of them vote. Although I know of no statistical records on Vietnamese voting patterns, my informants told me that Vietnamese immigrants do not participate in local and national elections. Minh, a forty-five-year-old immigrant, explained that Vietnamese people in France consider themselves to be foreigners and have little interest in French politics. The leaders of political organizations were the only ones who saw the Vietnamese community as a political force in France.

The high rate of naturalization among Vietnamese immigrants and refugees stems from their pursuit of personal benefits like employment, rather than from the desire to participate in French politics. Among the first and second wave of Vietnamese immigrants, many had already obtained French citizenship before they arrived in France.

The students from North Vietnam who came to France after 1954 as Vietnamese citizens later applied for French citizenship. But for many of them like Mai, a fifty-year-old doctor, it was a painful decision to make. She explained that she finally became a French citizen after twenty years because it was difficult to travel through Europe with a Vietnamese passport. She said that she held onto her Vietnamese citizenship for sentimental reasons. Mai felt that giving up her Vietnamese citizenship was separating herself from her past but also abandoning her country. Pierre, a thirty-two-year-old engineer who arrived in France in 1973, said that he was forced to give up his Vietnamese citizenship in 1979. After finishing his studies, he could no longer return to Vietnam and had to look for a job in France. He explained that in his field businesses require employees to be French citizens.

Vietnamese refugees have also applied for French citizenship after three years of residence in France. Ho, a thirty-four-year-old refugee, points out that being French had some advantages in terms of job opportunities. He explained that many naturalized refugees were able to work as civil servants in the French government. The few people I met who had not yet applied for French citizenship told me that they were not sure that they wanted to stay in France. Some of them were thinking about going to the United States for better job opportunities or to join relatives. They said it was easier to apply for immigration to the United States with a refugee status than as French citizens.

Vietnamese Migration to France

Bourdieu, a French sociologist, has suggested that immigrants arrive in their country of adoption with "capital," which can be defined as education, economic class, social status, or religious and cultural traditions that are advantageous in the new country (discussion with Bourdieu, Paris, September 1984). I suggest that, in addition, Vietnamese immigrants arrive with political "capital." Since their first migrations to France, Vietnamese immigrants have been heavily involved in political activities that paralleled the continuing conflict in their homeland. Each wave of immigrants brings its own capital of political experiences to bear on the Parisian political forum. The first wave experienced the indignity of French colonialism, the second the bitterness of American intervention, and the third the disillusionment of life under communism. The membership and strength of the two Vietnamese political factions have risen and fallen accordingly.

First Wave: Pre-1945 Immigrants

Immigrants of the first wave were nationalists who stayed in France for political or economic reasons. They were involved in political organizations that opposed French colonialism, and promoted Vietnamese nationalism. They considered themselves temporary immigrants and hoped to resettle permanently in Vietnam. In fact, in the early twentieth century, Vietnamese migration was temporary. Few Vietnamese chose to stay in France. There were three distinct categories of immigrants: workers, students, and military personnel. During the two world wars, the French government recruited Vietnamese workers as replacements for French workers who had left for the battlefields and as soldiers for French national security. During World War I the number of temporary Vietnamese immigrants in France was about 48,955, most of whom returned to Vietnam after the war (Hemery 1975; Le Huu Khoa 1983). In 1939, in contrast, the French colonial government in Vietnam was having difficulty recruiting Vietnamese men. Although the French government's goal was originally to recruit eighty thousand men, it fell far short of this with only twenty-eight thousand (Le Huu Khoa 1983). There were daily reports in Vietnam of draft resistance by the Vietnamese (Huynh Kim Khanh 1982).

On the eve of World War I, the French recruited mostly in Vietnamese villages. Although the villagers were officially given a choice about whether to enlist in the French army, in practice they had no such choice. According to a French bureaucrat's letter in January 1916, the mandarins were forcing villagers against their will to enlist in the French army, even resorting to physical violence (Le Huu Khoa 1983).

Coming from rural settings, most of these men had little or no education. Typically, they could not read or write even their own language. When the war was over, most of them went back to Vietnam. Only a small group decided to remain in France. Nam, a seventy-year-old retired factory worker, did not want to go back, suspecting that he would face unemployment in Vietnam. Because he wanted to be an artist, he thought it best to remain in France. He went to Paris where he painted Parisian scenes and sold his paintings to people on the street. Nam took a job as an unskilled worker in a Parisian factory after he married a French woman. He had to give up painting, as he needed a stable job to support his family.

Among the Vietnamese students who went to France after 1922, there were two distinct groups: students of wealthy families who had been sent abroad to study, and students who had received a French scholarship to pursue their studies. The French government hoped to instill a feeling of French identity in the young Vietnamese, but the result was quite the opposite (Gibson 1988). Many Vietnamese students became politically active against colonialism when they realized that the grand ideas of liberty, equality, and fraternity proclaimed at the French Revolution did not apply to the colonized peoples. According to Marr (1981), the number of Vietnamese students sent to France by their families to attend high school in the mid-1920s was increasing due to the pressure from French families in Vietnam for racial segregation in the high schools. Governor-General Pasquier came to realize that young Vietnamese were leaving the colony for political as much as for scholastic reasons (Marr 1981). For example, after the student strikes of 1926–1927, when the atmosphere in many colonial schools was tense, going abroad to study was the only way out for many young men. In 1930, after Vietnamese students were arrested during an anticolonial demonstration in Paris and some of them were deported to Vietnam, the French government was more successful in reducing the number of Vietnamese students in the metropole (Marr 1981). In spite of French efforts to promote better schooling in Vietnam, Vietnamese students who wanted a higher education went to France. The University of Hanoi was the only indigenous institution of tertiary education open to Vietnamese students seeking to pursue their studies beyond high school. Marr (1981:39) notes that the University of Hanoi provided a mishmash of advanced secondary, technical, and vocational schooling. Van, a seventy-year-old retired doctor, described the university's deficiencies:

> The university was only a three year program. The degree we received was not fully recognized in the job market. For example, with my medical degree I could practice in Vietnam only under the supervision of a French doctor. So I went to France to study for four more years to get a more reputable medical degree.

Since the University of Hanoi did not give a diploma comparable to the one from French universities, the only option for Vietnamese students who wanted genuine higher education was to go to France (Hemery 1975).

After graduation, most students returned to Vietnam. Van, for instance, went back to Vietnam to practice medicine but then returned to France after the Geneva agreement in 1954. The few who did not return stayed in France for personal reasons. Tran, a sixty-five-year-old retired engineer who had been planning to return to Vietnam, graduated during World War II and could not leave France. Instead he started working for a French company and eventually married a French woman.

Firsthand experience with the French indigenous population played a major role in the integration of the first wave of Vietnamese immigrants into French society. Upon their arrival, immigrants discovered that the French at home were different from the French colonists in Vietnam. Once in France, my informants commented that they felt free from the social stratification imposed by the colonial regime. Tran, for instance, who arrived in France in 1932, said he was surprised that most of the French did not treat him the way the French in Vietnam had. He said that when he arrived in France, he felt that he was treated like a man. For instance, he did not have to show deference and make way for Frenchmen. Nam, a seventy-year-old man who arrived in France

in 1942 as a soldier, also recalled the difference between French behavior in Vietnam and in France. He explained that in Vietnam,
the Vietnamese were treated as inferior, whereas in France,
French people did not look down on them just because they were
Vietnamese.

Many of my informants and informants' fathers of this generation married French women. As they told me, the Vietnamese
community in France at that time was small and consisted primarily of young men. Ho, a seventy-year-old informant, recalled that
there were not very many Vietnamese women living in France and
that he had to marry a French woman if he wanted a family. Ho
felt that he could not share his political life with his French wife and
children because they had not lived in Vietnam and knew nothing
about Vietnamese politics. Neither did he speak Vietnamese with
his children at home. He points out that since his children were
born of a French mother and raised in French society, they did not
need to learn how to speak Vietnamese. Tro, another informant,
had different motivations for marrying a French woman. He
wanted to marry a woman who was a political activist. He stated
that in Vietnam, the women he encountered were not interested
in politics and had the values of middle-class French colonist
women. He married a French woman from a working-class background who was a member of the French Communist party.

The community life of the first wave of Vietnamese immigrants revolved around political organizations. These organizations were primarily composed of men, to the exclusion of women
and children (see chap. 3 for a discussion of the evolution of political organizations in the Vietnamese community). As Ho and Tro
recalled, these gatherings were very important for keeping in
touch with the situation in Vietnam and for organizing political activities.

These early Vietnamese immigrants found improved job opportunities in France. In Vietnam, Vietnamese people could not
obtain well-paying jobs in the French colonial bureaucracy, and
were underpaid in other jobs. In France, even when working in
factories, they were getting higher salaries than in Vietnam. By
saving money, they were able to buy small businesses like restaurants in Paris.

Second Wave: 1954–75

After the Geneva agreement in 1954 and the withdrawal of French troops from Vietnam, a number of Vietnamese emigrated to France. They were "rapatriés," or people holding French citizenship. Among them were many Catholics from the north who feared religious repression from the communists. Unlike the third wave of immigrants, they did not hold a refugee status because they were French citizens. In addition, there were students from both the south and the north going to France to pursue their studies. My informants in this group were Vietnamese middle-class men and women and members of the UGVF.

The second wave of migration changed the existing Vietnamese community by including Vietnamese women and families. In the period 1954–75, the Vietnamese newcomers did not want to be integrated into French society. The fifth arrondissement in Paris became the area where many Vietnamese students lived and gathered together in Vietnamese restaurants of the neighborhood.

The fifty Vietnamese people of this generation whom I interviewed recalled that the community during that time was extremely politicized and that they had little interest in French society. For instance, Tuan, a thirty-five-year-old member of the UGVF, explained that he, like many other Vietnamese students in Paris at that time, had no French friends and little contact with the French people. He devoted all his time to the organization's political activities and to his Vietnamese friends. Since they were planning on returning to Vietnam after the end of the war, the students chose their studies according to what skills were needed in Vietnam, such as medicine and engineering. After the end of the war, however, most of these former students did not return to Vietnam (see chap. 5). Today, disappointed that they cannot go home, these Vietnamese have had to accept the fact that they are no longer temporary immigrants. Manh, a forty-year-old librarian who arrived in France in 1954, said that in the last ten years he came to realize that he would have to spend the rest of his life in France, and yet he knew nothing about French society. These immigrants are still involved in the political and social activities of the UGVF aimed at building support for Hanoi in the Vietnamese community. Having received French diplomas, they were able to enter the French job market, and now are concerned about their own careers in French society. In chapter 5, I will show how this generation of Vietnamese immigrants remains actively involved in Vietnamese political organizations.

Unlike the first wave of immigrants, many of my Vietnamese informants of this generation married within the Vietnamese community. Marie, a thirty-year-old chemist, told me that she met her husband in a political meeting of the UGVF.

Third Wave: The Post-1975 Refugees

Third-wave immigrants are refugees who fled Vietnam after 1975. My informants were members of anticommunist organizations. Like the first- and second-wave immigrants, they believe that their situation in France is temporary. I estimate that one-third of the refugees who arrived in France have little education and do not speak French. Their motivation for departure depends on a number of factors: involvement with the South Vietnamese government before 1975, social status, economic class, and religion. A number of Vietnamese intellectuals who today are leaders of political organizations have firsthand experience with the communist regime in Vietnam. These leaders, whom I interviewed, explained to me that they wanted to stay in Vietnam and cooperate with the communists. For them the communist victory meant the end of the war with its corruption and killings. Tuan, a sixty-year-old former professor at the University of Saigon, described his relief at the communist takeover: "I saw it as the beginning of peace in Vietnam. I am not a communist, but a nationalist. I did not want to leave Vietnam, because I wanted to participate in making Vietnam a better country." Nam, a forty-five-year-old architect who studied in France and returned to Vietnam to work in 1972, explained that he stayed in Vietnam after the fall of Saigon because he wanted to rebuild the country. He said that he disagreed with the communist ideology but thought that the country needed him.

After some time in Vietnam under communism, however, all of these people changed their minds. Three months after the fall of Saigon, Tuan wanted to leave Vietnam. It took him six years to get out. He worked for a French university and applied for a visa at the French Consulate. Tuan, however, gave up on getting an exit visa and decided to escape in a boat. He bought a fishing boat and planned his escape with some friends. Their departure was due to terminal disappointment with the communist regime. Nam had retired by the time the communists took over. He observed the social changes that were shaping the new Vietnamese society. He recalled:

> It was not the kind of society I had expected. We were tightly controlled by the Vietnamese government. An agent was appointed to control the activities of individuals in each neighborhood. Any so-called suspicious activity was reported to the authorities. We could not travel as we used to. We had to have a resident card and a special permit to visit friends and relatives. For me, the freedom we fought for had lost its meaning. I realized that soon even our minds would be under the control of the state.

Manh, a forty-year-old faculty member in the department of architecture at a university in Ho Chi Minh City (Saigon), decided to stay in Vietnam to rebuild the country. A year later at a faculty meeting, he realized that he could not work under a communist regime. He still vividly remembers the day when his faculty was asked to participate in a major project to relocate the population of Ho Chi Minh City to economic zones. Manh said that he was terrified by the project and protested, telling the officer in charge that it was impossible to move a large urban population in a few months. The officer responded that if the Cambodians had done this, so could the Vietnamese. Manh felt that the Vietnamese authorities wanted the experts' approval but not their advice.

Hoc, a sixty-five-year-old former journalist, had a similar experience. He wanted to stay in Vietnam after 1975. Throughout his journalistic career he said that he supported the communists by writing a number of articles for them. After 1975, however, he lost his house, though unlike many people he was able to keep his car. At the beginning he believed that he could work under a communist regime. Hoc said that he did not mind living with little as long as he was able to stay in Vietnam with his family. Trouble arose when he refused to let his son be enlisted. He said he started fighting with the local authorities about this matter, but soon realized it was a lost cause. He applied for an exit visa, which he obtained a few years later after pressuring the Hanoi government to let him leave with his family.

In the anticommunist organizations, there are also former South Vietnamese military officers for whom life under communism was a harsh experience. These individuals are the most outspoken opponents of Hanoi. Whereas Parisian Vietnamese intellectuals proposed compromises with Hanoi, these former military officers believed that Vietnamese freedom could be obtained only through military force. Life in reeducation camps had a dramatic impact on these people. The story of Lam, a forty-seven-year-old doctor who served in the South Vietnamese army, is the best example. He commented:

> When the communists took over I was sent to a reeducation camp for three years. The camp was the most horrible experience I have ever had in my life. The camps were run by uneducated people who had little understanding of Marxist ideology. We were treated like animals, and told we were not human beings yet. I am a doctor but I was forced to do manual labor. I became very sick and missed my family, who sent me packages of medicine and food without which I would not be alive today.

When Lam finished his time at the camp, he escaped Vietnam by boat with the aid of his family and friends.

Another category of refugees is composed of young men who have escaped Vietnam to avoid the draft. Tuan, a twenty-five-year-old member of an anticommunist organization, said that he was working as an electrician. He was asked to enlist, but he refused to do so. He lost his job and spent three years in hiding. He traveled from city to city carrying a false identification card, protected by friends and relatives. His family sent him the money he needed to survive. Finally he decided to leave Vietnam with the "boat people."

Other young men chose to escape because of the lack of upward mobility in the new society. Manh explained that because his father was an officer in the South Vietnamese army, he was not permitted to go to the university. He felt that he had no place in Vietnam because of his family's middle-class background. For five years, he worked as a small vendor on the "black market," but it was not something he wanted to do for the rest of his life. One day, at his brothers' suggestion, they decided to escape.

Other refugees left for fear of religious persecution. Catholics feared for their lives. Nga, a thirty-year-old woman, remembered that after 1975, many churches in Vietnam were closed down and a number of priests disappeared. She commented that her family was not involved in any kind of political activities, but she got scared when a friend who was also a Catholic was killed for no apparent reason. Concerned about their safety in Vietnam, Nga and her family applied for an exit visa to France, which they received before too long since her father was already a French citizen.

These refugees in France were treated far differently from first and second waves. Unlike the latter, these refugees were no longer part of a small, essentially invisible Asian community. Indeed, since 1975, the population of the Asian community in Paris has dramatically increased. According to statistical data from the Minister of the Interior, it is estimated that in 1962, seven thousand Vietnamese had arrived in France, in contrast to thirty-five thousand in 1980 (Le Huu Khoa 1983). This community consists not only of Vietnamese but also of ethnic Chinese from Southeast Asia, who live in ghettos like the thirteenth and the nineteenth arrondissements of Paris where they have their own Asian businesses. Most of the Parisians I met during my year of fieldwork complained to me about what they called the "Vietnamese invasion" and their "taking over" of native districts. Futhermore, as previously mentioned, in 1984 there was a strong anti-immigrant movement in France. "Le Front National," led by J. Le Pen, has exploited this sentiment for its own political gain. Every day I discovered new posters sponsored by the National Front covering the walls of Paris with slogans like "La France aux Français."[6]

After their ordeal of escaping Vietnam for freedom, the refugees arrived in France with great expectations. Soon after their arrival, however, they became disillusioned because instead of being welcomed, they were received with hostility. I spent a great deal

---

6. France for the French.

of time with the Vietnamese newcomers at the Mission Catholique, where they were offered French classes to facilitate their adaptation. When I asked them how they were adjusting to life in France, they all complained about the attitudes of the French people toward them and said that French people were racists. For instance, Nga, a thirty-five-year-old refugee who came to France, described an incident that set the tone:

> In 1982 a few months after I arrived in Paris, I went to the post office to mail a package. After I walked out the door, an officer ran after me screaming that I had tried to steal money from the clerk. I was shocked that I had been singled out as the thief just because I was Asian. It was humiliating. The next day I had to return to the post office and plead with the postmaster. Even today it hurts me to think about it. The situation could easily happen again.

Nga's experience is not an isolated case. Mai, a forty-three-year-old woman who arrived in France in 1984, had a similar experience. She commented:

> The first day I was in Paris I went to a store with a friend of mine. We did not buy anything. I started to leave the store from the wrong exit. Suddenly, I was grabbed by two men who accused me of stealing. I told them that I did not speak French very well and had misread the sign. They searched my bags for stolen goods. I was badly shaken up by the experience and did not leave the house for days.

Unlike those in the first and second waves of immigration, the refugees of the third wave of Vietnamese in France have encountered great difficulty getting jobs. In 1973, France suffered an economic crisis that lasted until the mid-1980s. The French economic situation affects the integration of refugees into the job market, but it affects the educated and uneducated differently. Among the educated, those with French degrees are better off than those trained in Vietnam. The educated include intellectuals, professionals, and former students. The intellectuals and professionals who studied in France and received a French diploma were able to find jobs in their areas of expertise when they arrived as refugees. Nam, who got his architecture diploma from a French university, found a job in his field as soon as he arrived. Vietnamese-educated professionals and intellectuals sometimes had to pursue further studies to obtain the French equivalent of their degree, or work as unskilled labor in French factories. Tuan had to study three more years at the Medical University of Paris before he could open his own medical office. Ho, a former schoolteacher who did not have the necessary degree to teach in French elementary schools, is now employed as a factory worker. Former students in Vietnam were able to continue studying upon their arrival in France. Many of them became engineers and found jobs in the computer industry. Tuyen and Lam were both high school students when they left Vietnam in 1975. In France, they studied computer science, and today both of them work for a computer business. The uneducated refugees joined the unskilled labor force in the French automobile industry. For the last twenty years the unskilled labor force in French factories has been composed of immigrants.

The increasing number of refugees who arrived in France after 1975 do not participate in the already established Vietnamese community's social life. Leaders of Vietnamese anticommunist political organizations have constantly warned the refugees that the established community is controlled by a communist organization affiliated with the Vietnamese Communist party. These leaders of anticommunist organizations promote the polarization of the community into political and social divisions.

The Boundaries of the Vietnamese Community

Social and political networks form the cultural boundaries of the Vietnamese community. Indeed, political structures serve as the foundations for all socio-cultural organizations within Vietnamese enclaves because the Vietnamese community is itself so cohesive. In its basic values the closely knit Vietnamese community relies on an institutionalized social order dictated by Confucianism. In fact, Confucianism still continues to influence the behavior of Vietnamese immigrants and refugees. Filial piety is one of the main principles underlying the Confucian morality of the family (Phan

Thi Dac 1966). In the Parisian Vietnamese community, the institution of the family provides one of the most explicit examples of
this cultural heritage. The family (*gia-dinh*) still has as central a
place in the community's life as it had in Vietnam. There is a
strong sense of solidarity among members of the same family that
also provides a valuable support for the Vietnamese. Phan Thi
Dac (1966:23) states:

> Cette solidarité réelle est donc un soutien précieux pour le
> Vietnamien, mais elle constitue en même temps de véritables
> chaines qui l'entravent dans toute son activité.[7]

The Confucian extended Vietnamese family is a source of security
because each individual has rights and obligations toward other
family members. If the father is no longer alive, there is always
someone in the extended family to take his place to fulfill his obligations toward his children. At the same time, filial piety involves
certain constraints such as taking the parents' advice for important
decisions regarding one's own life, and being responsible for their
welfare when they get older. Phan Thi Dac (1966) argues that the
Vietnamese pay great attention to kin blood ties. No one abandons
a kinsperson who has the same blood; any one who becomes successful in life has to share his fortune with his kin, and the family
shares the responsibilities and shame brought about by a blood
kinsperson's mistakes (Phan Thi Dac 1966).

De Vos (n.d.:1) argues that the most important feature of
Confucianism is "a sense of belonging and the moral cultivation
necessarily attendant upon particularist sentiments of fealty and
reverence directed toward family lineage and temporal authority."
He suggests that even though the Confucian doctrine is no longer
explicitly taught as such, the notion of belonging to a "quasi-
religious family" still persists in Japan. Among Vietnamese immigrants and refugees, I found a belief system much like that
which De Vos describes in Japan, in which Confucianism is inherent in all social relations and individual behavior. The Minh-

---

7. This real solidarity is thus a precious support for the Vietnamese individual, but
it also constitutes at the same time veritable chains which impede him in all his activities.

mang's first rule,[8] for instance, defined the individual's proper behavior according to his or her place in the social hierarchy.

The speaker identifies the listener according to his or her hierarchical position. The use of kinship terminology in all social situations expresses the relationships between people. A man is
called *chu* (uncle), an older man *bac* (older uncle), a woman *co*
(aunt), an older woman or married woman *bac* (older aunt), and
a younger man or woman (teenager) *chau* (child). As previously
stated, these terms are forms of showing respect toward others.

The Vietnamese system of patrilineal descent has been constructed with reference to Chinese prototypes. It diverges from the
Chinese system, however, in regard to the inheritance rights of
women. As in the Chinese legal code, the Gia Long code states that
each family belongs to a lineage whose ritual head is the senior
male, a direct descendant of the lineage ancestor. But in the 1400s,
the T'ang legal codes gave daughters as well as sons the right to in-
herit the land of their deceased parents and recognized the property rights of wives as well as husbands (Woodside 1971).

Vietnamese kinship terminology shows the complexity of
relationships. The terminology takes into consideration age, sex,
and relation to ego, ego's father, or mother. In ego's generation are
chi (female), *anh* (male), or *em* (younger male or female), which we
commonly call cousins and brothers/sisters in our European kinship system. In the parental generation, mother's younger sister is
di, mother's younger brother is *cau*, mother's older sister is *da*,
mother's older brother is *bac*, father's younger sister is *co*, father's
younger brother is *chu*, father's older sister is *bac*, and father's older
brother is *bac*. In the grandparental generation, father's mother is
ba, father's father is *ong*, father's mother's younger brother is *ong
cau*, father's mother's younger sister is *ba co*, father's mother's older
brother is *bac*, father's mother's older sister is *ba bac*. Father's
father's younger brother is *ong chu*, father's father's younger sister
is *ba co*, father's father's older brother is *ong bac*, and father's father's
older sister is *ba bac*.

This kinship terminology is no longer taught to the younger

---

8. The Minh-mang's first rule of behavior was that respect should determine proper
behavior in the hierarchical relationships between sovereign and subject, father and son,
husband and wife, and older brother and younger brother (Woodside 1971).

Vietnamese generation. Man, a forty-year-old immigrant, pointed out that children learn the terminology by generation without making any distinction between their mother's and their father's lines of descent. For example, the grandparents' siblings are called *ba* (female) and *ong* (male), and the parents' siblings are called *chu* (male), *co* (younger female sibling), and *ba* (older female sibling). He attributes this simplification of the language to the fact that most immigrants' children do not live in an extended family as they would have if they had been in Vietnam, and therefore there was no need for them to learn all the proper kinship terms.

Kinship terminology is also used outside the family. According to Anh, my Vietnamese professor in Paris, who was a linguist from the University of Hanoi, this terminology is also used today in the Vietnamese Communist party. Whereas *dong chi* (comrade) is used in Party meetings, the term *chu* (uncle) is often used to address one's superior in informal situations. For example, Ho Chi Minh was often referred to as *chu Ho* (uncle Ho) or *bac Ho* when he was an older man. I discovered a similar pattern in Vietnamese political organizations. Members call each other according to their places in the social hierarchy. For instance, among the youth in the UGVF, Vietnamese terminology has been replaced by French terms because many of the French-born Vietnamese speak little or no Vietnamese. I remember when I went to a picnic organized by the Youth Organization of the UGVF in May 1984 and found that the young Vietnamese were calling male adults *oncle* (uncle in French), female adults *tante* (aunt in French) and their peers *anh*, *em*, and *chi*. When I asked one of my informants, Mai, the reason for using this kinship terminology in a political organization, she explained that the organization was like a big family. Similarly, in the anticommunist organizations, young people called their peers *anh*, *em* and *chi* and the elders *chu* or *ba* even though they were not kin-related. Thus the use of kinship terminologies is intentional because it identifies the organization as a familial institution whose purpose is to reinforce ties among its members.

Vietnamese society contrasts with French society in that social life is based on the principle of collectivism as opposed to individualism. Dumont (1977:4) contrasts the concept of collectivism, which he calls "holism," to that of individualism:

On the one hand most societies value, in the first place, order: the conformity of every element to its role in the
society — in a word, the society as a whole; this is what I call
"holism." On the other hand, other societies — at any rate
ours — value, in the first place, the individual human being:
for us, every man is, in principle, an embodiment of human-
ity at large, and as such he is equal to every other man, and
free. This is what I call "individualism."

Dumont (1977) argues that in "traditional societies," like India and China, social relations take precedence over individuals,
whereas the opposite is true for Western society. Vietnamese immigrants and refugees in Paris organize their lives around the
ideology of holism. Hence Vietnamese individuals identify themselves in relation to their families. DeVos (n.d.) suggests that Confucianism shapes people's behavior toward the development of a
self that is socially rather than individually oriented. The Confucian rules of ethical conduct govern social behavior on the basis of
filial piety, brotherly submission, loyalty, trustworthiness, hu-
maneness, right conduct, politeness, and knowledgeability
(Woodside 1971). Kim, a sixty-year-old refugee, explained that at
an early age, the Vietnamese learn to behave in a social situation
according to these rules. In a discussion, for example, one should
never express anger even though the topic may be upsetting. Individuals should not hurt someone else's feelings, and should try
to ease tensions by being polite and pleasant. He points out that
loss of self-control is like loss of face. He believed that silence was
a way to avoid conflict and added that silence was also a form of
communication. Marie, a thirty-year-old French-born Vietnamese woman, criticizes Vietnamese social behavior that prevents individuals from expressing themselves. As a psychiatrist,
she said that she has been in therapy for many years to find her
own identity. In her family, conflict was always avoided, and she
felt that she could never talk to her parents about her own problems in an open discussion. As she said: "I grew up not knowing
how to be angry, or how to express my feelings. In therapy, I am
discovering myself all over again and I am learning to assert my
personality regardless of anyone else's feelings."
Because of her psychiatric education, it would clearly be un-

fair to say that her case was representative of the French-born Vietnamese. However, I met several French-born Vietnamese women who reported being in conflict with their mothers over their duty as daughters. Suzanne, a twenty-seven-year-old student, said that she visited her family very seldom because of her mother. Her mother, who disapproved of her allegedly frivolous life-style (having boyfriends and not being married), took the opportunity of her visits to pressure her daughter to change. But I found that 90 percent of the French-born Vietnamese that I interviewed had very good relationships with their parents. Indeed they showed a great deal of pride in their cultural heritage.

The unity of the family is best symbolized by the ancestral cult. In Vietnam, the ancestral altar carrying the ancestral tablets has a prominent place in each household. The eldest son of the family is responsible for taking care of the altar by offering joss sticks, drinks, and food to the spirits of his ancestors, as well as for organizing a feast for the whole family to celebrate the anniversary of each kinsman's death. Vietnamese women, however, can also assume the responsibility of the ancestral cults. If the eldest son is too young, the widow will perform the rituals and if there are no sons in the family, the daughter will have to fulfill this obligation (Phan Thi Dac 1966). According to Vietnamese beliefs, death is not a real departure from the family because a person is still present in the form of his or her spirit. The ancestral spirits remain actively involved in the lives of family members. They punish or reward family members according to their fulfillment of filial responsibilities. The rites of propitiation of ancestral spirits functioned to reinforce kinship ties.

In Paris, every Vietnamese household I visited had an ancestral altar on a chest in the living room. The altar did not consist of ancestral tablets, which, informants told me, had remained in the family village back in Vietnam. Instead, the altar included pictures of the ancestors modestly framed, a basket of fruit to feed the spirits, and joss sticks. Children are taught to care for the ancestral altar, especially the oldest son of the family. Manh, a thirty-five-year-old refugee, told me that every night he asks his six-year-old son to light joss sticks. But in Minh's family, in which there is no son, the oldest daughter is asked to perform this duty.

The pattern of family reunions for the anniversary of relatives' deaths is a bit different from that in Vietnam. First of all, these reunions are not held separately for each relative, but rather once or twice a year for all the dead collectively. Minh explained that in France, family members do not live close to one another and it is more convenient to gather the whole family a few times per year to celebrate all of these anniversaries at once. Secondly, it is no longer the responsibility of the oldest son to organize these reunions. Manh points out that sometimes the oldest son does not have a big enough apartment to invite the whole family, or the money necessary to throw a large dinner party. Hence family members share the responsibility for the ancestral anniversary and take turns gathering the whole family in their apartment.

The Vietnamese community is also kept close-knit through endogamy. Most of the Vietnamese immigrants and refugees I encountered said they prefer their children to marry within the Vietnamese community. Immigrants of the first and second wave who married French people told me that they would prefer their children to take a Vietnamese spouse. Minh, a forty-year-old immigrant woman married to a Frenchman in Vietnam, said that, even though she had no regrets about her own marriage, she wanted her daughters to marry Vietnamese men. Parents, however, do not openly pressure their children on the choice of their respective spouses. But Anne, her older daughter, points out that the pressure is more subtle. While her mother never commented much about her first relationship with a French boyfriend, she was very supportive of her second relationship with a Vietnamese boyfriend. She encourages her to see him more often, and when he visits the family, she treats him like a son. Anne also told me that her mother has already called his mother and they are both already making plans for the wedding.

Endogamy is also reinforced by social and cultural organizations. The UGVF, for example, organizes a summer camp for its youth every July. The camp enables Vietnamese teenagers to become acquainted. Anh, a French-born twenty-seven-year-old, like a number of other young men I encountered, met his wife during summer camp two years earlier. Both the UGVF and the anticommunist organizations have dance parties and picnics for their young members. Young women go there with relatives or friends.

The attitude toward mixed marriage among Vietnamese youth varies. While some of them are against it, others think that marrying either in or outside the Vietnamese community is acceptable. For example, Yves, a twenty-five-year-old student, pointed out that it is better to marry within one's own racial group. He argues that family ties are more important for Vietnamese people than for the French. He says that his parents, for instance, like to visit their married children frequently and take part in their lives. He believes that having a French wife who might oppose his parents' frequent visits would be a constant source of conflict for the couple. He points out that for his parents' sake, he would not marry out, even though they will not interfere with his decisions. On the other hand, Yvette, a twenty-two-year-old second-generation woman, is open to marrying either a Vietnamese or a Frenchman. She says, "It will depend on who I fall in love with. I will not limit my choices of a husband because of cultural differences."

Parents, however, do pressure their children to get married. Whereas young Vietnamese men feel that getting married and having children on their own is among their duties toward their parents, marriage is a constant source of conflict between young women and their mothers. Marie, a French-born thirty-two-year-old, explains that a woman has to be married in order to have status in Vietnamese culture. But like their French counterparts, many educated young Vietnamese women do not want to get married in their early twenties. Marie, for example, comments that even though she is a doctor working at a hospital, she is not considered an adult in her family because she is not married. Alice, a French-born twenty-nine-year-old, comments that even though her two older sisters are unmarried, her mother pressures her, but not her sisters, to get married. As a secretary, Alice does not depend on her family for financial support. She lives by herself in a Parisian apartment that she refers to as her own space. She said that every time she visits her family, marriage is a constant source of conflict between her and her mother. Alice is not dating anyone and does not know if she will ever get married because she believes that she will lose her freedom if she does so.

Athough in Paris most married couples live together in a single household, being separated from one's spouse has not created any instances of divorce among those I interviewed. Marie, a forty-year-old woman, has been separated from her husband for over a year. He found a better job in Bordeaux, but they decided it was more desirable for his family to remain in Paris since their three children would be attending the university in a few years. Yue, a thirty-year-old woman, has been married for five years and her husband left for Vietnam two years before I knew her. Although she has not seen him since, they write each other regularly. She told me that he wanted to remain in Vietnam for some time and she did not want to live there.

Phan Thi Dac once told me that it was not unusual in Vietnam for a husband and a wife to be separated. This was especially the case during the Vietnam War, when the men went to fight and it was some years before they could return home. She also pointed out that sometimes a man would marry another woman wherever he was stationed and afterward return home with a new wife. This was the case for her neighbor in North Vietnam, who, after fifteen years in the North Vietnamese army, returned home with a second wife and two children. She said that it took the whole family a couple of years to adjust to the new situation. According to Phan Thi Dac, in the past it was fairly common for the mandarins to be polygamous. Today in Vietnam, although polygamy is no longer legal, it is still practiced, especially among the generation of Vietnamese who went to the war. In my own research among Vietnamese refugees in Hong Kong, the United States, and France, I also found that it was still practiced. I have met a number of men who left Vietnam without their whole nuclear family, leaving behind their wife and a couple of children. In the new country, they have remarried while still supporting and caring for their first wife and children back in Vietnam.

In other instances, separation rather than divorce has been the alternative chosen by the Vietnamese older generation as a way to maintain the family unit. According to Manh, a sixty-year-old Catholic, marriage is a life commitment that cannot be dissolved. He was separated from his wife twenty years ago. Anh, a fifty-nine-year-old Buddhist man, has been separated from his wife for fifteen years. They were already separated in Vietnam, but they both decided to leave Vietnam after 1975 for the good of their children. Today Anh lives in Paris with two of his daughters, while his wife lives in Marseille with their three youngest children.

Anh told me that he was on good terms with his wife, but they did not get along in close quarters and thus it was best for the whole family that they not live together. They see each other, however, every three months for family reunions. Since he considers himself the head of the household, Anh financially supports the whole family, including his wife, but they both share the responsibilities of educating their children.

With some exceptions, Vietnamese immigrants living in France are surrounded by kin. They very often choose where to stay, or choose to move to a certain city, to be closer to family members. According to my informants, the Vietnamese population in France tends to be centralized around a few cities. I met a number of refugees who had moved to Paris even though they were originally resettled in other cities by the French government for purposes of employment.

The family forms the core of an important social network on which Vietnamese immigrants rely for material and moral support. Kin members help each other out with money, jobs, and living accommodations. In Vietnam, the extended family tends to live in the same village, the same district, and often in the same house (Hickey 1964; Phan Thi Dac 1966). The family, also called *ho*, was an extended family that included all members of a patrilineal descent group. The Vietnamese used the term *nha* in reference to their home. *Nha* does not simply mean "house" in the sense of physical structure. It implies the household group, the hearth, or the center of the individual's world-concept, reflected in the endearing words *nha toi* used by a young husband to address his wife, or in the term a villager uses when he refers to things such as land as *cua nha* (belonging to the household). The household may include grandparents, uncles or aunts, unmarried daughters, or eldest sons with their wives and children.

In Paris, the living situation of the immigrants has altered their traditional living patterns. Undersized Parisian apartments cannot accommodate a large Vietnamese family. The shortage of available apartments in Paris prevents displaced family members from living close to one another. The Vietnamese tend to follow the Parisian life-style of living in a district that corresponds with one's social class. The Vietnamese upper class lives in the sixteenth arrondissement, a French upper-class neighborhood, whereas the middle class lives in the fifth, fourteenth, and fifteenth and in the southeast suburbs. The lower class lives in the northern suburbs, working-class neighborhoods mostly made up of immigrants. While the Vietnamese do not live in ghettos, they rely on restaurants and grocery stores owned by Vietnamese and Chinese refugees from Southeast Asia in order to eat or purchase traditional fare and enjoy the ethnic ambience of these places. On Saturdays, the fifth and thirteenth arrondissements are crowded with Asian shoppers, especially Vietnamese, who come from all over Paris to do their shopping for the week. The Vietnamese tend to shop only in those stores that carry the ingredients necessary for Vietnamese cuisine. In fact, in all the Vietnamese households I visited, Vietnamese cuisine is standard for meals. Cooking is performed mostly by women, but I was invited to single men's homes and they were able to cook as well. When I asked them if they cook French food, they replied that Vietnamese cuisine was easier to prepare and tasted better. Minh said that once in a while during the week she cooked French food like steak and French fries for lunch when she did not have time to prepare a proper meal. When they eat out they go to Vietnamese restaurants and seek the best ones in the city. Working bachelors, young Vietnamese men, and students take their meals in cheap Vietnamese restaurants where one can get *pho* (Hanoi-style noodle soup) or other Vietnamese specialties for not too much money.

The family network provides emotional and financial support for the Vietnamese immigrants and refugees. Family members help each other a great deal to live in French society.

Since it is very difficult to find an apartment in Paris, Vietnamese immigrants and refugees rely on their kinship networks for living accommodations and sometimes, like the French, try to beat the French institutions. Nga, a twenty-two-year-old French-born woman, for example, lives in an apartment complex reserved for French civil servants. She got the apartment from her sister who is a civil servant, and who had moved out a year earlier to the suburbs without informing her office. Ho, a fifty-year-old man, lives in a similar situation. Having been in Paris for only a couple years, he was not eligible for a "low-income" housing facility. His cousin, who had a large two-bedroom apartment in the complex, moved out a few years earlier and gave Ho his apartment without informing the "low-income" housing office. As Ho points out, "The French think that we Vietnamese all look alike and the manager of the building did not notice when I took over the apartment of my cousin."

Other Vietnamese immigrants and refugees live in apartments owned by relatives. Minh, a thirty-five-year-old refugee who arrived in France two years ago, lives in the apartment bought a few years ago by her sister, who was sent to the provinces for her job. Annette, a thirty-year-old French-born woman, lives in the apartment of her father, who moved to Canada.

Vietnamese immigrants and refugees also use networks to find jobs and advice for professional training. Anh, a forty-year-old refugee man, found a job at a relative's store. Tuan, a twenty-five-year-old computer engineer, advised his younger cousins to get a degree in computer science because he believed that he would be able to help them find a job with his professional connections. Nga, a forty-year-old refugee, found a job from her doctor brother-in-law who had a friend working in a medical laboratory in Paris.

The family also provides emotional support for immigrants and refugees. A great many of their social activities revolve around their families. For instance, Minh, a thirty-year-old divorced refugee who lives alone with her three children, spends a great deal of her time with relatives. Minh explained that she has not been able to make friends among the Parisians since she arrived three years ago. She comments that her sisters have been helping her adjust to her new life in France. If she has a problem, she calls them up because they will be able to help her out. Once in a while, she goes shopping or takes walks with them in Paris. The weekend is a time when her sisters' husbands help her with the education of her children. They give her advice about which social activities they should participate in and which studies they should pursue. One Sunday Anh, her eighteen-year-old son, was the subject of discussion. Anh was not doing well in school because, unlike his brother and sister, his French was not good. One of his uncles told Minh that Anh should be sent to a boarding school. He believed that Anh did not have enough opportunity to practice his French, and being away from home would force him to focus on his studies. Minh took this advice.

A typical Parisian Vietnamese household is composed of parents, grandparents, unmarried children, and one or two close relatives. Many of my informants live with one or two relatives, an elderly parent, or a refugee relative who needs a temporary or permanent place to stay. When the apartment is too small, they throw mattresses on the living room floor for the extra members of the household or add more beds in the bedrooms. Tro, a fifty-year-old immigrant, said that he did not mind sharing space with relatives and friends. He pointed out, "We [the Vietnamese people] like to share what we have, even though it is not always convenient." Tro is married with three young adult children and lives with his mother and a young relative in a three-bedroom apartment in the suburbs. Everyone participates in the household. His wife and mother are responsible for maintaining the house and preparing the meals. Tro, his older son, and the relative provide financial support for the household, while his younger son pursues studies at the university and his daughter is finishing high school. Tro does not want his younger son to work. He believes that it is the responsibility of the whole family to support him while he is in school.

Elderly Vietnamese do not live alone. They either live with their children or have relatives living with them. Indeed, their children have a duty to care for them. As mentioned earlier, Confucian doctrine emphasizes children's filial piety toward their parents. I have met a number of Vietnamese of the second wave who had requested exit visas from Vietnam for their elderly parents. Nga, a thirty-five-year-old immigrant, explained that she applied for an exit visa for her mother because her older sister could no longer care for her in Vietnam. Nga argued that she wanted her mother to leave Vietnam for family and not political reasons. She got pretty upset when her mother, upon her arrival in Paris, was asked by French government officials to apply for refugee status.

The family network is international in scope and is used not only for support but also for financial assistance. Most Vietnamese immigrants send goods to relatives in Vietnam. These goods are then sold on the black market for cash. A great deal of income is spent on purchasing goods for kin back home in Vietnam. Minh, who returns to Vietnam every summer, has a list of items she needs to buy beforehand. I was astonished at the number of goods she had accumulated in her kitchen over the year: rice cookers, sewing machines, and fabrics. She is proud to tell me that she spent a great deal of money on the purchases. Ho, a thirty-year-old business executive, resents the high expectations of him by his family back in Vietnam. He says that they know he is doing very well, and every year they demand more and more goods. This year, his mother asked him to send a photocopier in order to establish a small business. Ho says that even though he is doing well, he still has to support his wife and child, and his mother is totally unrealistic about his life.

The network extends to other family members living abroad in the United States, Canada, Australia, and other European countries, and there is constant movement between these countries. For example, Hai, a twenty-five-year-old student, was planning on going to the United States to live with his sister. After spending a month with her in the summer of 1983, he found that the Vietnamese in the United States had better opportunities. Manh wanted to go to the United States to marry the cousin of his friends who had visited Paris that spring. Suzanne regularly visited her two sisters, one of whom lived in England and the other in West Germany.

The Vietnamese principle of sharing with relatives extends to adopted children of relatives still living in Vietnam. The adopted children are not treated differently from the other children of the household. Indeed, as Hickey (1964) reports, adoption is common in Vietnam when a couple does not have any children or has only daughters and wants a son to maintain the lineage. Even though the reasons for adoption are now quite different, it remains a widespread practice among Vietnamese immigrants. An immigrant family may adopt children from siblings living in Vietnam to help the family economically and to give these children a better education. Since 1975, for example, thousands of unaccompanied children have left Vietnam as "boat people." They were sent by their parents to relatives, uncles or aunts, living abroad. In other instances, Vietnamese immigrants returning to Vietnam to visit have taken relatives' children back with them to France. Nga, for instance, adopted her brother's four youngest children (ages three, eight, ten, and twelve) because he was unable to support his family of eight in Vietnam. She points out that since she is not married and makes enough money as a professor, she can help her brother out by raising his children. Nga believes that adopting children from one's own family is different from adopting orphans. She comments that her adopted children are aware that their actual parents live in Vietnam. And even though they call her mother, they know that she is their aunt who cares for them. She said that she expects them to write to their parents and visit them with her during the summer. In my recent fieldwork among Vietnamese youths in Oakland, California, I have met a number of Vietnamese adolescents who were living in the United States with a relative, either an uncle or an aunt. Although they missed their parents, who had stayed in Vietnam, they spoke highly of their adoptive parents. Since the adoptive parents are siblings, they are in contact with the natural parents and keep giving reports on the progress of the child. Anh, a seventeen-year-old boy who came to the United States a few years ago as an unaccompanied minor, told me that his uncle had been doing his best to give him an education.

Although the family remains the core of Vietnamese cultural identity, political divisions in the community have created a new set of social relations and cultural identities among its members.

The Parisian Vietnamese community is, of course, highly political. Even though I estimate that only one-third of the Vietnamese immigrants are members of political organizations, politics permeates all social institutions (see chaps. 5 and 6). Thus politics is also found in the Vietnamese family.

Political division within a family is very common among Vietnamese immigrants and refugees. It is part of the legacy of the Vietnamese war of over forty years. In the families of most of my informants, some relatives had joined the Vietnamese communist forces (Vietminh), while others had supported first the French and later the South Vietnamese government. In the north, the division of Vietnam in 1954 had a terrible impact on family members who were separated. Ho, a fifty-year-old immigrant, returned to Vietnam after 1975 and saw, after over twenty years of separation, his brother, who had joined the Vietminh in 1952 when Ho was leaving Vietnam to pursue his studies in France. Manh, a fifty-five-year-old refugee who had worked for the South Vietnamese government, joined his sister in Paris in 1976. His sister, who had left Vietnam as a student twenty years earlier, has always been a strong supporter of Hanoi. I also found that, in the same family, half of its members living in the United States were involved in anticommunist organizations while relatives in Paris were members of the UGVF. Yet despite these political differences, and the bitterness of the war, the family unit remains untouched. As I was often told, family bonds cannot be untied, because members are united by the same blood. Even today, in family gatherings politics is not discussed, especially if some members are still involved in political organizations. I would argue that politics as a taboo topic reflects the Confucian social ethics that govern family life. No one wants to bring up this topic because it may offend other members or provoke a conflict when it is a time to celebrate.

In the community, however, politically opposed family members avoid each other. Van, a thirty-year-old member of the UGVF, was told by his aunt, a member of an anticommunist organization in Geneva who identifies Van as a communist, not to visit her. Khoa, a twenty-five-year-old member of the UGVF, recalled the time when he was sitting in a coffee shop on campus and saw his cousin with friends putting up anticommunist propaganda posters on the university's walls. Khoa and his cousin did not greet each other and pretended not to know each other. The case of Khoa best illustrates the dual status of Vietnamese in their community, as both family members and members of a political organization. In a public setting, Khoa's behavior demonstrates his loyalty to his political organization rather than to his family.

Chapter 5

The Pro-Hanoi Faction

The pro-Hanoi political network is monopolized by a single political organization, the Union Générale des Vietnamiens en France, or UGVF (Hoi Nguoi Viet-Nam Tai Phap). The UGVF is the largest organization of its kind and enjoys official recognition from the government of Hanoi.

The Structure of the Organization

The UGVF represents a long-established community that is considered today to be an elite group among immigrants. These are the first and second waves of immigrants and the first generation born in France. As former French university students, members often have access to prestigious jobs. The elitism of the organization is best described by Xuan, an eighteen-year-old first-generation immigrant who commented:

> It is an exclusive organization composed of upper- and middle-class immigrants. In order to be accepted in their social circle one has to have excelled educationally or in the job market. Otherwise you are looked down upon and people will ignore you.

My informants from the organizations were women and men whose ages ranged from seventeen to sixty-five. They were well-educated university students, university professors, engineers, doctors, and civil servants.

The UGVF also has a number of working-class Vietnamese immigrants from the first wave who have formed their own subgroup within the organization. As former leaders of the organization, they still have a voice in decision making. As in a Vietnamese family, the elders are well respected both for their contribution to the organization and for their advice.

The UGVF itself consists of: (1) officers, including a president, a vice-president, and a secretary; (2) active members, organized into eight specialized subgroups; and (3) the supporters or passive members. Officers are elected every three years.

I found some similarity between the structure of the UGVF and that of Vietnamese communist society. According to a visiting professor at Jussieu University, Vietnamese society today is organized into three main social groups: (1) the Vietnamese Communist party; (2) the Chi-Doan, unions such as the women's union and the youth union, whose membership is based on merit; and (3) the Phan-Doan, professional organizations for people who have the same occupation, such as doctors, professors, or engineers. I have compared these categories with the UGVF and found striking parallels. The UGVF is a union in which there are several subunions, including the Youth Union, within the communist organization and seven other Phan-Doan corresponding to different professions.

According to my informants, the UGVF is not a Vietnamese communist organization even though some members belong to the French Communist party. Only a few UGVF members belong to the Vietnamese Communist party. Membership in the Vietnamese Communist party is based on merit. It was explained to me that one has to be presented by other members of the Party and then one's membership is voted on by the members. However, many of my UGVF member informants were members of the French Communist party. Unlike membership in the Vietnamese Communist party, membership in the French Communist party is quite simple. All one has to do is just apply to be accepted.

The UGVF organization is financially supported by its members through donations. Because of the organization's strong ties with the French Communist party, it has access to a number of social benefits. For instance, in the spring of 1984, I was invited to a picnic organized by the Union des Jeunes Vietnamiens en France, UJVF (Union of Vietnamese Youth of France). The picnic took place in a private park outside of Paris. The park was open exclusively to members of the French communist labor unions.

Political meetings of the organization are generally open to members. I was told that each subgroup holds its own meeting every three months. Subgroup members participate in a "congress" to select new leaders and discuss political issues. Even though I had never been invited to any organizational internal meetings, I was invited to and attended the UJVF Congress in the spring of 1984.

The organization has its headquarters in Paris but also has offices in major French cities like Marseille, Lyon, and Bordeaux. The headquarters in Paris is located on the ground floor of a building in a Parisian residential district. From the outside the building looks like any other building in Paris. I was surprised to find an automatic security entrance. After entering the first door, I had to announce myself before being allowed to pass through a second, glass door. This was clearly not an ordinary office. The only other times I had gone through this type of security in Paris were at a bank and at the Vietnamese consulate. This security system symbolizes the climate of insecurity in the Vietnamese community. I was told later that the UGVF's leaders were afraid of attack from the anticommunist organizations. The violent attacks by these organizations on pro-Hanoi Vietnamese in the United States are well known to UGVF members. When I first told my UGVF informants that I wanted to go to the headquarters, they warned me that there was nothing for me to see or do there. They were quite right because the rare times I went there for an interview, I only met the few people who worked in the organization's administration. Inside, there was a large but modestly furnished conference room that is mainly used for meetings. In the basement were lodged the headquarters of the newspaper *DoanKet* and the UGVF secretary's office. It was not a social gathering place.

DoanKet is the official monthly magazine of this organization. The forty-page magazine contains articles on both the overseas Vietnamese community and Vietnam. Written in the Vietnamese language with a few pages in French, its stories cover the community's social activities, performances in such arts as theater, dance, and music, politics and economics of Vietnam, and economic cooperation between France and Vietnam. In the last two pages, there is a calendar of social and cultural events for the following month, with a small space devoted to advertisements for organizations affiliated with the UGVF, such as Chua Truc Lam (a Buddhist institute in Villebon-sur-Yvette), and forthcoming events in the community. The political overtones of the magazine are most evident in articles on Vietnam. Hanoi is never criticized. Instead, its political actions are justified. *DoanKet* not only gives the Vietnamese immigrants information, but also reinforces the political solidarity of UGVF members with the government of Hanoi.

DoanKet used to be sold in all Vietnamese-owned stores. Since the arrival of the recent refugees, however, many store owners refuse to sell it because they do not want to risk losing their refugee customers who would boycott stores associated with Vietnamese communists. In fact, the Vietnamese refugees are extremely fearful of the UGVF because of its alliance with the Vietnamese Communist party and do not want to participate in social organizations allied with the UGVF, which they called a communist organization. A few years ago, "Thanh Binh," one of the first Vietnamese businesses in the fifth arrondissement, became the target of anticommunist propaganda. Gossip concerning the owner's affiliation with the Vietnamese communists was circulated throughout the refugee community. To put an end to the propaganda, the "Thanh Binh" manager decided to sell only anticommunist newspapers. Today *DoanKet* is sold only in those Vietnamese bookstores with a UGVF affiliation, such as the bookstore Sud-Est-Asie in the fifth arrondissement, at the UGVF's headquarters, and through subscription.

The organization also offers its members a special discount airfare to Vietnam. This was a business deal with Air France, which flies weekly to Vietnam. While the regular round-trip airfare from Paris to Ho Chi Minh City is about one thousand dollars, the UGVF offers the same trip for about seven hundred dollars. One has to be a French citizen and a member of the UGVF in order to qualify. I was told that a number of refugees who took on French citizenship have become UGVF members in order to take advantage of the discount. The two most popular times to travel are in early February for the New Year celebration, Tet, and for a month's vacation during the summer. In fact, many Vietnamese immigrants like to join their families in Vietnam to celebrate the new year. In the summer, most Vietnamese immigrants in France, like all French working people, have a month's vacation, and many of them want to use this time to visit relatives in Vietnam.

The social gathering place for UGVF members is a restaurant called the "Foyer des Etudiants Vietnamiens" (Vietnamese Students' Center). It is located on Monge Street in the student district, within walking distance of the major Parisian universities. There is no sign outside of the building to indicate the existence of a restaurant, which is simply the ground floor of a six-story building, surrounded on all sides with large windows covered with curtains. One has to have been given the address or to have been there before to know that it is a restaurant. The "Foyer des Etudiants Vietnamiens" was previously a cafeteria run by a Vietnamese student cooperative, but is now owned by a Vietnamese family. It is a place where first-generation Vietnamese go to see friends and feel part of the community. It is also an important political center. The restaurant is most frequented at lunchtime. Inside, the restaurant seats UGVF members separately from other customers. UGVF members, especially young people who are students and former students, sit at the two large tables to the left of the room. The Vietnamese who do not want to share their meal with everyone else, and the French customers, are seated at small tables to the right. On the second floor is a small meeting room with a TV, a bar, a few chairs and tables, and a large bulletin board advertising all the latest social and political activities. This room is mostly frequented by Vietnamese students who use the bulletin board to inform others about such activities as skiing, picnics, and demonstrations. On the bulletin board I have also seen clippings from newspapers on subjects such as French racism. The "Foyer des Etudiants Vietamiens" is to a certain extent the headquarters of the organization, where everyone catches up on community gossip.

Organizations Allied with the UGVF

Since 1975, the UGVF has established a large social network in the Vietnamese community. The number of social and cultural associations affiliated with the UGVF has increased since 1978. Whereas the leaders of the UGVF wanted me to believe that these organizations were not part of the UGVF, I found out that they were all organized by members of the UGVF. The UGVF, which competes with anticommunist organizations for the refugees' support, used these social organizations to indirectly increase its membership. These associations cover religious, social, and cultural activities and maintain autonomy vis-à-vis the UGVF. Even though they have their own budget and leaders, they often rely on the UGVF for sponsorship. The social associations offer the UGVF members a wide range of activities such as picnics, ski weekends, summer camps for families and youths, and evening parties. These associations, such as Loisirs Vacances Franco-Asiatiques, do not publicly acknowledge their affiliation with the UGVF, but it is a matter of common knowledge.

The Buddhist institute Chua Truc Lam in Villebon-sur-Yvette (a small town southwest of Paris) was started as an independent organization and is now associated with the UGVF. Manh, the fifty-year-old head monk of the temple, who has a doctorate from the Sorbonne, explained that before 1975 the overseas Buddhist organizations were involved in the peace movement in South Vietnam. He said that they were very much opposed to Diem, the South Vietnamese military junta, and American military intervention. Today, however, UGVF ties are so powerful that the Buddhist institute is now a subgroup of the UGVF. The head monk also pointed out that Chua Truc Lam was also associated with the Buddhist institute of Hue. He himself is the leader of the Overseas Vietnamese Buddhist Association. At the temple he was assisted by two young monks who had arrived from Vietnam two years earlier.

When I asked Manh if he had any contact with the other Vietnamese temple monks, he replied that he did on occasion, but secretly, to talk about religion. He explained that some of these monks were involved in anticommunist political activities. Fearful that he would upset his members, he did not want such meetings to be public. When I asked him what would happen if a young man or woman from the Parisian Vietnamese community wanted to become a monk, he replied that he would send him or her to be educated and trained at the Buddhist institute in Hue. He believed that Paris did not have the right environment for a monk to be trained. He said that he himself goes back to Vietnam for short visits.

The construction of the new building of Chua Truc Lam was started in 1980 after the abandonment of a French government-sponsored project to build a new Buddhist temple for all Asian people in Paris. Because of political divisions within the Vietnamese community, the Buddhist laity were opposed to the project and refused to participate in religious rituals with members of the opposing faction. When the project was abandoned, UGVF members decided to build their own temple, which they financed through donations.

In 1984, even though the building was not quite finished, religious rituals were still held every Sunday. Located in a residential area, it is a magnificent building modeled on the temples in Vietnam. On the first floor is a large reception room with a kitchen in the back. On the second floor is the main ceremony room dominated by a large statue of the Buddha. I was told that the statue was donated by the Vietnamese government in Hanoi. During the week, the temple's activities are few, but on Sundays, it is very active. Every Sunday the monks perform two services, one in the morning and the other in the afternoon. The participants are usually Vietnamese elders of the community. For special occasions, like the first moon, the New Year's celebration, one hundred participant families and their children go to the temple to celebrate. None of the women wear traditional dress but rather the latest French fashions. Between services, the women are busy in the kitchen preparing a vegetarian lunch and chatting. The men gather in the main conference room drinking tea and talking, and children generally play in the garden. When lunch is served, everyone finds a place at the two large tables set up for the occasion. There is always plenty of food. On these occasions, members of the Vietnamese consulate are invited to participate. It was here that I first met the cultural attaché of the consulate, who later invited me to the consulate for tea. I always enjoyed going to the temple because I was often mistaken for a Eurasian. The older women would order me around in Vietnamese just as they would have addressed any first-generation Vietnamese woman.

Although every Vietnamese in the community is free to participate, very few refugees go to the Chua Truc Lam temple. I remember one Sunday meeting when a thirty-five-year-old refugee woman had come to the temple with her husband and her two children. She told me that it was her first time at the temple. She had come out of curiosity. During the service break, she remained seated with her children, while her husband was off by himself in the garden, smoking a cigarette. I knew that she was a refugee by the modest way she dressed and because no one was talking to her. She commented that while her husband felt very uncomfortable in a crowd of pro-Hanoi supporters, she did not care. Nonetheless, she said that she did not think she would return.

Les Catholiques Progressistes is another religious organization associated with the UGVF, representing Catholics who are pro-Hanoi. The group consists of three hundred members, headed by a Vietnamese Catholic priest, Father Michel. Unfortunately, he never agreed to an interview with me. They have their own headquarters and Sunday services, but I was not invited to participate. A few years ago, the organization was banned from performing services at the Mission Catholique des Vietnamiens in Paris because of political conflict within the congregation. The priest, who was asked to resign, later formed his own congregation. I was told that one source of the conflict had been the priest's opposition to the publication, in the monthly Catholic magazine, of political materials directed against the Hanoi government.

Leadership and Membership

Leaders are elected every two years by organization members. There is one leader for the whole organization, who works closely with the leaders of each subgroup. The leaders do not necessarily belong to the Vietnamese Communist party. I was told, however, that some of them were members, but no one knew exactly who or how many. The former president of the UGVF, Nguyen Khac Vien, for instance, is today living in Hanoi and works as the editor-in-chief for the Vietnamese publishing company called Les Editions en Langues Etrangères (Nguyen Khac Vien 1983).

Although most members deny that the UGVF's policy is dictated by Hanoi, I would argue that Hanoi does provide some kinds of guidelines for the organization. The organization, however, is not a front for the Vietnamese communists in France, but rather acts as a supportive overseas political organization with policy that remains close to that of Hanoi.

The leadership of the 1984 UGVF was primarily composed of intellectuals. Retired workers and former political activists still have a role in the decision-making process of the organization. I was told that they are often consulted for advice on how the organization should deal with the Hanoi government. One member pointed out that they were from the same social background and belong to the same generation as the current leaders in Vietnam. He pointed out that before submitting any proposal to Hanoi, they try it out first on the elders in order to find out if it is worth sending.

To be a member of the UGVF, one pays the annual fee to obtain his or her membership card and a subscription to the magazine *DoanKet*. There are two kinds of members at the UGVF, activists and supporters. The active members belong to one of the eight subgroups, organize cultural and social events, and participate in meetings. Among the supporters, I found two different categories: (1) people who become members in order to benefit from the UGVF and (2) former activists who no longer wished to be actively involved, but want to show their support for the organization. One of the main advantages of belonging to the UGVF, as I mentioned earlier, is the special discounted airfare to Vietnam.

Since 1975, the arrival of large numbers of refugees has added a new dimension to the recruitment process of the UGVF. The UGVF is searching for a strategy that will appeal to the refugee population. Unlike the newly arrived Vietnamese refugees, the long-established community has gone through the adaptation process. They "know" that most of the refugees will not return to Vietnam. As Minh, a forty-five-year-old UGVF member, said:

> We have to help them face reality. From our own experiences we can help them adapt to French society. Many anticommunist political organizations are fooling them by insisting that they will soon be able to go back to Vietnam.

Under the slogan "building a Vietnamese community abroad," the UGVF is reaching out to the newly arrived immigrant community. French social service offices turn to the

UGVF, not the anticommunist organizations, for assistance with the refugees. As Minh said:

> It helps us get to know the refugees as individuals and let them know that we (the long-established immigrants) are not only interested in recruiting membership for the Vietnamese Communist party. We want to change the negative image that the refugees have of us.

In addition, the UGVF is organizing social and cultural programs in which newly arrived refugees and long-established immigrants can mingle. The programs do not advertise their affiliation to the UGVF in order to avoid alarming the refugees. One program that has been quite successful is the high school tutoring run on Saturday afternoons in a Parisian high school. I was told that refugees sent their children there because of the educational background of the tutors, but I was also told that some refugees had found out that the program was run by the UGVF and took their children out. In 1984, a friend of mine was working on a project for the creation of a new Vietnamese cultural center. The activities of the center were oriented to meet the needs of a young audience, with video games, sports activities, and a cafeteria. The UGVF places a special emphasis on youth since they will be the future members of the Vietnamese community.

The Role of the UGVF in the Community

The political aims of UGVF have changed over the years. Before 1975, the UGVF was almost exclusively a political organization. Its purpose was to hasten the end of the Vietnam War and to support the Hanoi government. One of its tasks was to gain the support of the French. Tuan, a forty-five-year-old librarian, recalled:

> Twenty years ago, when we were students, we devoted all of our free time to the "cause." We believed that our political work in France was necessary to resolve the conflict in Vietnam. If we were not in a meeting, we were papering Paris with posters and leaflets.

Suzanne, a thirty-two-year-old doctor, remembered going door to door keeping the French informed about the situation in Vietnam and soliciting signatures for an antiwar petition. According to most of my informants, they developed a sense of community and commitment through their involvement with the UGVF.

After 1975, when the war had ended and the two Vietnams were reunited, many members of the UGVF considered returning to Vietnam to participate in reconstructing their country, but the Vietnamese government considered such Western-educated intellectuals a serious threat. The new leaders in Hanoi were not intellectuals at all, but revolutionaries who were rewarded for their military successes with civilian rank. Additionally, Hanoi favored Vietnamese who were educated in the Soviet Union over those educated in France, Canada, and the United States, for it was thought that in the Soviet Union, Vietnamese intellectuals received a more politically compatible education, one more likely to contribute to the revolution. Only a few intellectuals who were officially recognized for their contribution during the war were invited to stay in Vietnam and teach at the university.

In Paris I met two Vietnamese scholars who had received their degrees in the Soviet Union. Tri, a Vietnamese visiting scholar at the University of Paris, had spent three years in the Soviet Union, where he received his master's degree in humanities. Today he is teaching at the University of Hanoi. Mai, a thirty-five-year-old student, had spent six years in Moscow, where she received her bachelor's in linguistics. In 1984, she was in Paris on a two-year scholarship to earn her master's.

Vietnamese immigrants who wanted to return to Vietnam could not find jobs comparable to the ones they already had in France. For instance, when Manh, a French-educated engineer, went to Vietnam to offer his skills, instead of being given engineering work, he was assigned to work in a rice field. Disappointed, he returned to France. The elderly Vietnamese immigrants, however, were able to return, and they retired in Vietnam. According to Manh, a sixty-five-year-old immigrant, they were first-wave Vietnamese immigrants who had arrived between the two world wars and had been unable to return to Vietnam because of World War II.

Since 1975, the role of the Vietnamese community in France has been redefined as indirectly contributing to the reconstruction of Vietnam. In France, the pro-Hanoi leaders no longer oppose a permanent community. As Ho, a forty-year-old member, explained:

> In the past, we did not want our members to integrate into French society because we thought they were needed in Vietnam. But since Hanoi's rejection of the French Vietnamese in 1975, our attitude has changed. Now we encourage the establishment of a permanent Vietnamese community in France.

Once the community was regarded as permanent, the political discourse of the UGVF changed. A primary objective became to maintain the cultural identity of the community in order to preserve a Vietnamese cultural heritage for future generations born overseas. Patriotism was redefined in terms of building an overseas Vietnamese community that supported Vietnam, and in particular the Hanoi government.

In their political discourse, UGVF members and leaders stress the importance of maintaining Vietnamese cultural identity. Knowing full well that they will never be able to return to Vietnam, the Vietnamese immigrants nevertheless want their children to preserve their cultural heritage. Cultural and social events are advocated as a means for extending a sense of collective identity. They also participate in French cultural events in order to become more integrated into French society as an ethnic group.

For many years the UGVF has run a Saturday school in Bagneux, a suburban town south of Paris. Here, Vietnamese children are taught Vietnamese language and culture. In the past, children were taught Vietnamese out of necessity. It was assumed that they would need to know the language when they returned to Vietnam. Today, youngsters are taught this language to preserve the cultural heritage of their ancestors. The Saturday school also strives to remind children of their cultural background. Educated in French schools, they do not always understand that they are different until singled out by French children as *chintoque* (a derogatory term for Chinese). The community tries to counteract the influence of racism by instilling in the children a sense of ethnic pride. Members of the UGVF who are very involved in the organization send their children to the Saturday school. But the school in Bagneux is very far away from Paris and some parents have given up on sending their children there.

The UGVF, like its anticommunist counterpart, sponsors special events to celebrate all the traditional Vietnamese holidays. Tet and the mid-autumn festival are the two most important events of the year. The Vietnamese celebration of the lunar new year, Tet, is the most popular and well attended event of the year. In Vietnam, Tet is primarily a family gathering to remember the dead and to reestablish ties with kinfolk (Hickey 1964). In the Parisian Vietnamese community, Tet not only is a family affair, but also reinforces the bonds among UGVF members. Indeed, everyone in the organization participates in preparation for Tet. This festival involves traditional Vietnamese plays and dances performed by nonprofessional actors willing to give their time for daily rehearsal two or three months before Tet. While watching the play and the dances, I was amazed at the talent of the performers who had no professional training.

Several months before Tet, the walls of buildings in several Parisian districts are covered with posters inviting Vietnamese immigrants and refugees to participate in the Tet celebration. The UGVF Tet is always the first celebration in Paris and takes place before the anticommunists' Tet festival. Expertly organized and financed by the UGVF, Tet is a spectacular display of Vietnamese culture. The UGVF members are always proud of their Tet, and one informant pointed out that Tet gets better every year. The Vietnamese ambassador is always invited and his presence is formally acknowledged by the master of ceremonies. No celebration can commence until he is officially welcomed and applauded. In his speech, the master of ceremonies sends his best wishes to Vietnam, hoping that the new year will bring a better economy and better relationship between Hanoi and Paris.

In 1984, the UGVF's Tet was held at the Palais de la Mutualité, a city hall in the fifth arrondissement. According to informants, a few years earlier there had been regular confrontations with members of anticommunist organizations in front of the hall where UGVF's Tet was celebrated. When I participated in UGVF's Tet in 1984, there was no anticommunist demonstration.

Instead, three buses of police were stationed in front of the building to assure the security of the participants and to discourage violence from anticommunists. For the occasion, the whole building
was decorated with colorful paper. An ancestral cult with a large
picture of the Buddha dominated the entrance hall and was surrounded by large plates of fruit donated to the ancestors. The fruit
had been flown in from Vietnam by Air France airlines the morning of Tet. The fruit came from different places in Vietnam:
grapefruit from Bien Hoa, coconuts from Ben Tre, watermelons
from Phan Thiet, and branches of a peach tree from Nhat Tan
(*DoanKet*, March 1984:15). In the hallways, every social organization affiliated with the UGVF had its own booth with materials on
its social activities. On the same floor, the auditorium was set for
the plays, music, and dances organized by the UGVF theater
group. On the second floor, a large room was set up as a restau-
rant/cabaret where a Vietnamese live band performed most of the
evening. In two other smaller rooms on the second floor, games
were set up in a video game room where young people and older
people gathered for the Chinese checkers contest.

By 6 P.M., the building was crowded. Vietnamese of all
generations participated in the celebration, from traditionally
dressed elderly women to the "punk" style members of the younger
generation. The atmosphere of the festival emphasized a return to
tradition and peace in Vietnam and in the community. Adults
mingled and greeted each other for the coming new year while
their young children ran about. There were a few French people,
spouses of Vietnamese with their Eurasian children. A few French
celebrities were invited by the UGVF, along with French friends of
UGVF members. Among the officials invited were the Vietnamese
consul general, the Vietnamese representative at UNESCO,
representatives of the French Communist and Socialist parties and
of the French Ministry of UNESCO and UNICEF, and major
diplomatic missions from different French cities and Parisian
districts.

The UGVF Tet celebration is always well attended by the
long-established Vietnamese community. There was, however,
also a small but noticeable post-1975 refugee presence. They were
mostly women and children. They did not mingle with the rest of
the participants but stayed together in a small group. I could spot

them easily because they did not speak much French and were modestly dressed. They did not participate in most activities going on in the building, but came to see the show and left soon after.

As mentioned earlier, the show was performed by the theater organization of the UGVF. The show consisted of traditional Vietnamese plays, *Hoi Xuan* (Spring Festival), *Xuy Van Gia Dai* (Van, the Crazy Woman), and *Tieng Dan Than* (The Magic Cithara), and music presented by 150 members of the UGVF. At 9:30 P.M. there was a play performed by French-born Vietnamese youngsters from the Bagneux Saturday school. While drinking and eating traditional Vietnamese food, the spectators sat and enjoyed the show.

After the show, families with children left, but others stayed around playing games or sitting in the restaurant. At 2 A.M. all the seats were removed from the auditorium, opening space for dancing until dawn to the disco music of a live band. The night was not only for the youth to celebrate. Older Vietnamese men were among those who stayed up all night drinking and chatting.

Another important cultural event is the mid-autumn festival *Tet trung-thu* for children. Huard and Durand (1954) suggest that the mid-autumn festival is one of the seasonal celebrations and represents the revenge of the female moon symbol over the male element. They note that mid-autumn is the time of engagements and weddings. In Paris the festival was organized by the Saturday school and took place on a Saturday afternoon at the "city hall" of Bagneux. Festivities began at 3 P.M. There were about six hundred participants, with children forming the largest portion. Children aged one to thirteen participated in the celebration. Some of the little girls wore traditional Vietnamese dress, colorful long silk tunics with white pants underneath. Children's games were organized by the Bagneux school, including games made up by the children as well as traditional games organized by the adults. At 4 P.M. a show, followed by songs, was presented by the Bagneux schoolchildren. Children from five to sixteen years of age performed in theater productions. It was very amusing at one point, when the five- and six-year-olds, on their best behavior, were singing on stage, to see two three-year-old girls, who had followed their siblings onto the stage, acting up and enjoying the attention they were receiving from the audience. Everyone in the room was laughing at the two young actresses. Even the young singers were having a hard time remaining serious. At 5 P.M. all the lights were turned off and the children, under the supervision of the Saturday school teachers, were given lighted, colored paper lamps (some representing animals) and paraded around the room singing. According to Huard and Durand (1954), people in Vietnam used to walk through the streets at night with lighted lamps. The event was attended by a delegation from the Vietnamese consulate, but no official speech was made to acknowledge their presence.

Both festivals not only display Vietnamese culture but also serve to strengthen social ties among members of the UGVF. These ties are reinforced during the preparation of these events, when members voluntarily give their time and talents.

As mentioned in chapter 5, the Vietnamese immigrants do not want to integrate into French society. In the discourse of the UGVF there is a problem with the French-born generation,[1] which does have loyalty to Vietnam but lacks the nationalist identity possessed by the first and second waves of immigrants. Instead, they have a dual French and Vietnamese identity.

To identify the Vietnamese as a French ethnic minority requires a reevaluation of the role of the Vietnamese community in French society. This issue was avoided by the first and second waves of Vietnamese immigrants. In fact, they focused on ties with Vietnam and ignored the French aspect of Vietnamese identity. The French-born generation, however, is concerned about its future in French society. These Vietnamese belong to a subgroup of the UGVF, the UJVF. They actively participate in building a French-Vietnamese community. They also assert themselves independently as a political force on the French political scene. Thus, in November 1984, the UJVF participated for the first time in a peaceful demonstration against racism, organized by the French Left (the Socialist and Communist French political parties). The demonstration mobilized thousands of youths, mostly of Arab origin, who claimed their right to participate in the increasingly racist French society. The march left Montparnasse at 2 P.M.

---

1. I have also included in the category of "French-born Vietnamese" those Vietnamese who were raised in France, since they portray themselves as having a dual French and Vietnamese identity.

and arrived at Republique at 8 P.M. Even though it was a cold and rainy day, the participants, mostly young people, were in good spirits, yelling slogans. The small delegation of the UJVF (twenty people) did not pass unnoticed by the French media. The whole group marched wearing yellow masks over their faces. Unlike the rest of the groups, the Vietnamese talked quietly to one another as they walked rather than yelling or singing.

In September, a month before the march, the UJVF organized a panel on pluralism and racism in France. The discussion lasted three hours. They had invited members of the coalition "Mouvement contre le Racisme et pour l'Amitié," a national antiracist movement. A forty-five-year-old senior member of the UGVF named Manh, a French woman member of the French Communist party, and forty members of the UJVF (from sixteen to thirty years old) were also present. One of the four panelists, all members of the UJVF, opened the discussion by giving the audience a brief history of the Vietnamese migration to France and their political participation in the Vietnamese conflict. Then Manh talked about his own experience as an immigrant:

> Before 1975, none of us thought that we would end up staying in France the rest of our lives. We believed that as soon as our studies were finished, we would return to Vietnam. We did not try to integrate into French society. There was them and us and we stayed among ourselves. During that time, French people considered us as foreigners and supported our antiwar movement in Vietnam. But now "les beaux jours sont finis" (the happy days are over). We are no longer visitors but immigrants. Racism is not yet directed at us, but it soon will be with the large numbers of Vietnamese and Chinese newcomers. So it is time to build a Vietnamese immigrant community and ally ourselves with other immigrant groups.

He concluded his speech with a warning to the audience that the rapid growth of the Parisian Asian community would result in severe discrimination against all Asians regardless of their origins and status in French society.

When the discussion was opened to the floor, the reaction

from the audience was mixed. Most of the young French-born generation said that they were unaware of French racism. As mentioned in chapter 4, the French-born Vietnamese belong to middle-class families and are themselves well educated. Only one twenty-year-old French-born woman said that she thought people in her office seemed to disapprove when she talked on the phone in Vietnamese. She said: "They do not like it because they cannot understand what I say and it annoys them." Another seventeen-year-old fellow told the audience that the discussion should also address Vietnamese racism toward others. He argued that the Vietnamese had the same racist attitude toward anyone who was not Vietnamese, especially the Chinese. He recalled the time when he crossed the street not to be on the same sidewalk with a group of young Chinese. People in the audience approved of his comments and added that this was a fair point to bring up in a discussion of racism.

One of the panelists pointed out that unlike the French-born generation of Vietnamese, the Vietnamese refugees were in the same situation as the Arabs, who also had little education and were thrust into the lowest social class. Their integration into French society was far more difficult than for Vietnamese youths who had been raised in France. He suggested that the UJVF create a committee to work with other antiracist organizations, to make the Vietnamese community aware of racism and to push their leaders into more open community dealings with the French.

This meeting reveals a strong lack of awareness among middle-class Vietnamese youths that they belong to an ethnic minority in France. While other nonwhite ethnic minorities in France, such as the Algerian youths, are already revolting against discrimination, the French-born Vietnamese have not yet felt concern about the issue of racism. To a certain extent, the French-born Vietnamese have integrated well into French society, in which social class has primacy over ethnicity. For example, they do not identify themselves with other ethnic groups who do not belong to the same social class. On the other hand, their integration into French society has been only partial since, like their parents, they have been primarily concerned with political issues regarding Vietnam.

The participation of the UGVF in French public events has

a lot to do with its affiliations with French political parties. During my fieldwork I noticed UGVF presence in social events sponsored by either the French Communist or Socialist parties. Every September, the French Communist party organizes a political fair, "la Fête de l'Humanité." The UGVF is always represented in such events. Traditionally, the Vietnamese booth is manned by the more senior members of its organization.

In other instances, the UGVF participates in multi-ethnic cultural events sponsored by French leftist organizations. In 1984, the Centre Culturel Georges Pompidou in Paris presented an exhibit entitled "Les Enfants de l'Immigration."[2] Even though the show was mostly concerned with the adaptation of French-born North Africans to France, the UGVF was represented by children from the Saturday school in Bagneux. On a Saturday afternoon, they performed a traditional Vietnamese play, *Le Génie des Montagnes et des Eaux.*[3] Members of the UJVF were also there to help set up the play.

The political discourse of the UGVF presents Vietnam as a Third World country that lacks job opportunities for Vietnamese people educated in the West. Instead of encouraging their return, the UGVF requests only financial aid and technical advice for Vietnam from the Vietnamese. Supporting Vietnam is thus one of the main goals on the UGVF agenda. The UGVF is involved with two major assistance programs: (1) the establishment of an import-export company and (2) the exchange of technical expertise, scholars, and artists.

The UGVF seeks to contribute to the reconstruction of Vietnam by sending experts on advisory visits. The "technical branch," formed by French-educated Vietnamese immigrant engineers, offers its skills to Vietnam. A number of these experts have been to Vietnam for short periods to work with their counterparts in rebuilding the infrastructure of the Vietnamese economy. These team projects are often part of fund-raising campaigns in the community. For example, the Association des Sciences et Techniques (Science and Technology Association) of the UGVF and a Vietnamese medical team jointly created a medical association in Viet-

---

2. "The Children of Immigrants."
3. "The Spirit of the Mountains and the Waters."

nam. The UGVF (*DoanKet*, June 1984:19) in the same year sponsored the creation of the Société d'Etude et de Réalisation de
Projets de Coopération Economique, or SEREPCO (Society for
the Study and Establishement of Economic Cooperation Projects).

The UGVF also sponsors cultural and intellectual exchanges
with Vietnam. A few times a year, Vietnamese cultural groups are
invited to perform in the major French cities. The UGVF organizes the tours and provides the necessary personnel. With the
assistance of the French cultural minister, Vietnamese cultural
groups were invited for a European tour in March 1984. The artists performed traditional theater and music and presented a puppet show on water. In Paris it was performed at the Maison des
Cultures du Monde and at the Maison de la Culture de la Seine-
Saint-Denis. The events in Paris were well attended by both
French and Vietnamese. In Marseille, however, the tour had to be
cancelled. The anticommunist organizations warned the mayor of
the city that there would be a large demonstration and possible violence if UGVF-backed cultural groups performed in the city. To
avoid conflicts and bad publicity, the UGVF cancelled the performance.

Vietnamese scholars are often invited to give lectures and
participate in symposia sponsored by the UGVF and the association l'Amitié Franco-Vietnamienne (Franco-Vietnamese Friendship Association). L'Amitié Franco-Vietnamienne is essentially an
organization of non-Vietnamese French intellectuals. It promotes
intellectual exchanges and technical assistance to Vietnam. Even
though it is a "nonpolitical" organization, its existence depends on
good Franco-Vietnamese diplomatic relations. Vietnamese scholars from Hanoi are invited to give classes and seminars on Vietnam at the University of Paris VII for a year or two. The University of Paris VII, in the fifth arrondissement, sponsors an exchange
program with the University of Hanoi. In fact, every year the
Department of Vietnamese Studies invites Vietnamese professors
to teach. They give classes on Vietnamese literature, history, and
language. There they are welcomed by the French and the French
Vietnamese professors (who are also members of the UGVF). One
of the Jussieu French professors told me that contemporary Vietnamese politics is never discussed in the classroom. He explained
that the Franco-Vietnamese exchange curriculum deals only with

studies of Vietnamese history, and thus avoids political confrontation between the Jussieu faculty and the invited Vietnamese professors.

The UGVF has also established a trade network with Vietnam. The UGVF set up an import-export company, Vina, in Paris in 1978. In Vietnam Vina's activities are supervised by the minister of foreign trade ("commerce extérieur"). In the beginning, Vina was run and financially supported by the UGVF, but it is now financially independent. Vina possesses a total monopoly on the trade of goods between Vietnam and the Vietnamese abroad. From Vietnam, it imports foods and artifacts. From France it exports the luxury items much in demand back in Vietnam. These goods are purchased by immigrants and sent to relatives in Vietnam.

Vietnamese artifacts, such as lacquered furniture, paintings, and art objects, are displayed in the store "Maison du Vietnam," located on a main street in the fifth arrondissement. Vietnamese and French alike purchase these expensive artifacts. Unlike the "Maison du Vietnam," "Vina-Paris" does not have an entrance onto the main street. Because it is located in the thirteenth arrondissement, access is difficult. One has to enter a courtyard to see the entrance. Inside, the store looks remarkably like the state-owned stores I encountered in the Republic of China. Two kinds of goods are displayed: foods imported from Vietnam and goods that will be exported to Vietnam. There is a wide range of items to be exported: Peugeot bicycles, stereo equipment, fabrics, and medicines. They will be purchased by Vietnamese immigrants to send to their families in Vietnam. These commodities are extremely valuable in Vietnam, where they are sold on the black market for cash. My informants often told me that instead of sending money to support their families, it is better to send commodities, which have a higher value on the black market. For instance, relatives often requested medicines. Because they are scarce, medicines have an enormous resale value. Vina passes on some of the discounts it receives from large French manufacturers. It offers its customers good deals, covering packaging and delivery of goods to Vietnam.

Vina also operates an air freight service and arranges freight shipments on the weekly Air France flight to Ho Chi Minh City.

In Vietnam, the recipients are notified promptly and Vina will hold the package up to one month for pickup. Each individual is allowed to receive three packages a year. Sending packages through Vina is safe, and shipments reach Vietnam faster than by the regular postal service. Refugees and immigrants alike use Vina's services. Because Vina is affiliated with the UGVF and Hanoi, anticommunist organizations have tried to boycott the business by telling refugees not to use Vina's services. In spite of this warning, many refugees use them. I went there a couple of times on Saturday afternoon and the office was crowded with Vietnamese refugees. In addition, Vina was able to subvert this boycott attempt by subcontracting its business out to Chinese-owned stores. These stores then acted as middlemen between Vina and the Vietnamese. Mention of these stores' affiliation with Vina was carefully avoided.

UGVF: Behind the Bamboo Hedge

An analogy can be made between the bamboo hedge of the nineteenth-century village and the political discourse of Vietnamese political organizations. Popkin (1979:90) explains:

> This sense of corporateness, of a community set against the outside world, was expressed in the large, dense hedge that surrounded each village. In an insecure country the hedge was a functional security measure, but beyond its protective value it was also a kind of sacred boundary of the village community, the sign of its individuality and its independence.

The UGVF political discourse is to the UGVF organization what the bamboo hedge was to the nineteenth-century Vietnamese village. It keeps strangers out, hides the organization's internal political conflicts, and unifies the members of the organization. The UGVF is still for many French people an unknown organization. UGVF members do not talk with strangers about their organization or its goals. Neither do they give information on its internal political struggles. Instead, the truth lies behind the bamboo hedge.

I would like to point out that although the UGVF is not

openly a communist organization, its political discourse is that of the Vietnamese Communist party. The organization's history of Vietnam represents the Vietnamese as a people who were able to maintain their own cultural identity and who for centuries have fought against foreign domination by Chinese, French, and Americans. Vietnam is presented as a free country under a communist government, and yet a developing country still coping with the effects of the last war. Vietnamese overseas immigrants are recognized as having indirectly participated in the Vietnamese revolution. As mentioned earlier, since the Vietnamese immigrants could not permanently return to Vietnam, their role in the reconstruction of Vietnam was chiefly to support the government of Hanoi. The contribution of the UGVF to Vietnam has been considerable. This organization collects donations when there is a natural disaster in Vietnam, individually finances relatives, and shares members' technical expertise by sending out engineers and doctors to Vietnam for a few months at a time. The newspaper *DoanKet* praises the contribution of the community to the rebuilding of Vietnam and the efforts of the Hanoi government to overcome the economic crisis. The newspaper always gives the reader a positive image of Vietnam without any mention of its troubles or criticism of its government. The presence of the Vietnamese consular delegation at all social and cultural events is a constant reminder of the political affiliation of the UGVF with the Vietnamese Communist party.

Although the fact is often denied by the UGVF leaders, the UGVF does compete with anticommunist organizations to recruit new members. As Van, a forty-five-year-old member, said:

> We are not concerned with the anticommunist propaganda. Anticommunist organizations are mostly composed of former South Vietnamese leaders who want to regain their power in the community. They are too busy competing with each other to gather the strength necessary to threaten our organization.

However, in the last few years the UGVF has resorted to deleting its name from advertisements for its cultural events in order to attract noncommunist refugees who are afraid of getting involved with an organization allied with the Vietnamese Communist party. The UGVF name was printed only in very small characters at the bottom of a poster advertising the 1985 Tet celebration. No sponsorship information was given on the poster announcing a performance given by UGVF children on a Saturday afternoon. In addition, the new cultural center in the fifth arrondissement was not publicized as being affiliated with the UGVF.

I discovered in 1984 that the UGVF's leadership within the Vietnamese community is threatened by a growing number of anticommunist political organizations. These political organizations constantly challenge UGVF's control of the community. In a discussion I had with a French scholar who was working on Vietnamese history and who had often visited Vietnam, I learned that leaders of the Vietnamese government are worried about the growing number of overseas anticommunist political organizations. Indeed the overseas Vietnamese community is an important asset for the Vietnamese economy, because so many Vietnamese immigrants and refugees send goods to relatives, send donations, lobby in Paris for amicable Franco-Vietnamese relations, and provide technical assistance and cultural exchanges.

The Vietnamese communists' coming to power has failed to fulfill the expectations of the Vietnamese immigrants in France. Indeed, the community has become very concerned about the future of Vietnam. The harsh reality of the communist regime has been reported by refugees and also experienced by Vietnamese immigrants on visits home.

In spite of all the reassuring political discourse by UGVF leaders, the members are losing faith in the government in Hanoi and the leadership of the UGVF. They find it difficult to believe that Vietnam's sagging economy is due only to bad luck or the legacy of the war. They wonder about the ability of the Vietnamese government to rebuild the country and question the role that the Soviets are playing. Many UGVF members had hoped that if they could not go back, they could at least participate in Vietnam's reconstruction. In this, too, they have been disillusioned. Minh, a forty-five-year-old woman professor, observed:

> With our skills and the support we had given all of those years to the revolution, we believed we had a contribution to make.

But as the years went by, we realized that Hanoi was not interested in what we had to say, and very soon we felt abandoned. Today, we still hold meetings, but we avoid discussing Vietnamese politics and focus on topics related to the economy without questioning our role.

Every year, Minh goes back to Vietnam to visit her family. She said that since the war has been over, she has been trying to help her relatives who are still living in Vietnam. She spent half of her income on goods necessary for their survival and sent them packages as often as she was allowed to do so. At the UGVF, Minh never missed a meeting. Though she listens to the agenda like the others, she said that she tries to keep a low profile.

Thus, many members like Minh still participate in the organization, but give top priority to their family life. Minh's case best illustrates how the immigrants' patriotism is now directed to their own families rather than to the Vietnamese Communist party, as was the case before 1975. Huynh Kim Khanh (1982) suggests that patriotism, which meant devotion to one's patrimony, rather than nationalism, was the main force behind the Vietnamese Communist revolution. I argue here that this same patriotism is the main force behind the attitude of many UGVF members. Without withdrawing from the organization, they reduce their participation in its political activities and devote more time and money to their own families still living in Vietnam. They are concerned about the politics of the Hanoi government because of its potentially negative impact on the livelihoods of their families. Minh told me that she always gave a donation when a natural disaster hit Vietnam even if none of her family lived in the area. She believed that such disasters could have happened where her family lives and she wanted to show her support for families caught in the disaster.

It is important to note that the members' hesitation to express themselves within the organization stems from fear of publicly or even privately criticizing the Hanoi regime. As I was told, if they openly disapproved of the policies of the Hanoi government, they might not be able to return to Vietnam and visit relatives. Minh pointed out that the government could refuse them entrance visas.

UGVF members like Minh do not want to leave the UGVF

but they wish that the UGVF had more autonomy from the Hanoi government. They want to create a Vietnamese community abroad that will be free from Vietnamese communist power. They want to support the reconstruction of Vietnam, but also have the freedom to question the Hanoi government's politics. When they engage in UGVF political discourse, they always refer to what Vietnam used to be and the role of the revolution.

While Vietnamese immigrants unquestioningly accept the leadership of Hanoi, the French-born Vietnamese are already clamoring for greater independence from the Hanoi regime. These malcontents represent the future leaders of the UGVF, so their opinions cannot be taken lightly. Thus the generations are locked in a stalemate. They are neither threatened with expulsion, nor do they leave. As in a village, the older members try to channel and control the younger ones, who endure this manipulation because they know that one day they will be the leaders. This generational conflict reflects an organization in transition.

Unlike their parents, the French-born UGVF members are openly challenging the political allegiance of the organization to Hanoi. Raised in France, with a dual French and Vietnamese identity, their loyalty is not only to Vietnam but also to the Parisian Vietnamese community. They want to know the truth about the socio-political situation in Vietnam, so they demand open discussion about it with the UGVF leaders. They question the current leaders' ability to evaluate the government of Hanoi objectively.

One of the best examples of this conflict occurred at a meeting to discuss the situation in Cambodia, organized by the UJVF in October 1984. The invited panelists were French scholars who had worked in Cambodia and Vietnam and a UGVF leader. The French scholars were leftists (some I knew were members of the French Communist party) and very much pro-Hanoi. The audience was composed of fifty people, mostly young French-born Vietnamese members of the UJVF. It was an open meeting so anyone could attend, but the people who showed up were only in the UGVF network. Also, a few older male Vietnamese members of the Vietnamese Trotskyist organization had invited themselves. I had been invited by a member of the UGVF who had asked me not to tell anyone at the meeting who had invited me. The two

French scholars, recently returned from a trip to Cambodia at the invitation of the Hanoi government, were working together on a book on Cambodia and gave a presentation on their experience in that country. They argued that there was no visible Vietnamese military presence in Cambodia and justified Vietnamese occupation of Cambodia by pointing out that after the Pol Pot regime, there was no one left in Cambodian society qualified to lead the country. The Vietnamese were thus helping Cambodians rebuild their country. They then explained the efforts of the temporary Vietnamese government to preserve Cambodian culture and emphasized that the Cambodian rather than the Vietnamese language was taught in school.

The discussion started when one of my informants, Phuong, a twenty-seven-year-old woman, spoke up from the audience. I should add that Phuong, a doctor, is considered to be an outspoken person even by the rebellious group within the UJVF. She stood and, holding a piece of paper on which she had a number of previously prepared questions, asked the panelists why the government of Hanoi never informed the UGVF community about what is going on in Cambodia. She pointed out that from 1976 to 1979 no one in the Vietnamese community in Paris knew what was going on in Cambodia. "Instead," she said, "we had to find out by ourselves in French newspapers." Then she suggested that the UGVF should request the true story from Hanoi on the Vietnamese invasion of Cambodia. She blamed the UGVF leaders and the government of Hanoi for misleading the UGVF members on the situation in Cambodia. She added that if Hanoi leaders were the only ones to blame for concealing information, then they needed to change their attitude toward the UGVF and better inform the Vietnamese overseas if they wanted the Vietnamese immigrants to support them. One of the French panelists replied that the government of Hanoi, like any other government in the world, was reluctant to give out information likely to jeopardize national security.

Another member of the audience asked if the Cambodians were governing their own country. The other French panelist reiterated that the Vietnamese presence in Cambodia was to help the Cambodian people rebuild their country. She pointed out that there was no sign of Vietnamese military presence in Cambodia and that the Vietnamese living there were mostly civilians working with the population.

Then an older Trotskyist Vietnamese man stood up and said that the Vietnamese invasion of Cambodia was comparable to the Russian invasions of Czechoslovakia and Poland. No one addressed his comment. He was asked to sit down and be quiet.

Finally Phuong stood up and said that she did not understand why thousands of Cambodians were leaving Cambodia if it was such a pleasant place to live. Her question was quickly answered by a leader of the UGVF who told her that, as in many other less developed countries, people left for Western countries to have a better standard of living and it had nothing to do with politics. I should point out that one Cambodian student had been invited by a UJVF member but his presence was totally ignored by panelists and audience alike.

After the meeting, Van, a twenty-six-year-old student, commented privately that he had been expecting such answers, which followed the UGVF party line. When asked why he bothered attending, he replied, "I did not go there to learn anything new. It is a step in the right direction just to bring this topic to an open discussion." The meeting was indeed a show. Everyone knew what to expect from the panelists and knew ahead of time that the meeting was purposely set up for a confrontation. In my opinion, however, it was a perfect opportunity for the French-born generation to show their disagreement with the UGVF leaders' total loyalty to Hanoi. They asked pertinent questions to provoke the panelists and the leader of the UGVF. The purpose of the meeting was also to set a precedent for dissent in the UGVF community. Phuong explained that it was one of the first meetings in which members were openly expressing themselves and requesting facts about the situation in Vietnam.

The rebellious attitude of the French-born generation is also expressed in *Bulledingue*, a monthly newspaper that the UJVF started a few years ago. The newspaper, written in French, publishes articles critical of Vietnamese life under the Hanoi government. *Bulledingue* is not available to the general Vietnamese public, but it is circulated inside the UGVF community. The editors limit circulation because they do not want the anticommunists to seize upon this as further evidence of Hanoi's flaws and to use it as propaganda against the UGVF.

Freedom of speech is the major theme of the newspaper. The second generation claims that the immigrant community should be free to express itself and to talk openly about Vietnam. Michel, one of the editors, commented that "we represent the majority of people in the UGVF, who are critical of Hanoi but afraid to speak up. We give them the opportunity to speak up and share their experiences within the safety of a closed network." For example, in one of the articles, "Revolution scientifique et pesanteurs culturelles," the writer blames the incompetence of the Vietnamese bureaucracy for the country's failing economy.

> Les dirigeants politiques, en majorité d'origine rurale restent coupés des détenteurs du savoir moderne (intellectuels et techniciens) . . . ils ont souvent decidé d'une manière volontariste et irréfléchie une planification qui ne tient pas compte d'un développement coordonné de la production et des besoins de la population. (*Bulledingue,* February 1984:5) [4]

I have met a number of UGVF members who have read *Bulledingue.* Some of my informants approved of the newspaper and felt that its editorial staff was very courageous to publish what everyone else thought but was afraid to say.

However, there is still pressure from the leaders of the organization to maintain group solidarity. A year later, the UJVF began publishing another newspaper, *Graffiti,* to back the political position of the UGVF. I was told that *Graffiti* was intended to compete with *Bulledingue* and force it out of business. While *Bulledingue* editors are considered to be the rebellious members of the UGVF who even refuse to sign their articles, *Graffiti* editors are model members. Written both in Vietnamese and in French, *Graffiti*'s articles focus on the Vietnamese community in France and its

---

4. The political leaders, of rural background, remain cut off from those who hold modern knowledge (intellectuals and engineers) . . . They decide spontaneously without planning ahead of time. Their decisions do not take into consideration the process of development and the needs of the population.

French-born generation. As one of my informants, an anonymous writer in *Bulledingue*, said, *Graffiti* writers want to become the future leaders of the UGVF.

In 1984, there was no sign that the internal conflicts provoked by some members of the UJVF would cause the organization to split. French-born Vietnamese felt a strong need to remain united and loyal to the organization. After all, they had been raised in the organization. Just as the nineteenth-century Vietnamese village was surrounded by a bamboo hedge, members of the UGVF are enclosed by the organization's political discourse. This is illustrated by the Fourth Congress of the UJVF, held at the Martin Luther King Building in Paris in April 1984. The meeting is held every two years in a French or other European city. Two hundred French-born Vietnamese between the ages of thirteen and thirty-five attended the meeting. The two-day meeting was held in a large auditorium with a podium and a large table. For participants, headphones were attached to each chair for a direct translation from Vietnamese to French. Many French-born Vietnamese did not speak Vietnamese. The purpose of having most of the speeches in Vietnamese was not to facilitate communication, since the majority in the audience did not speak Vietnamese. I would suggest that the use of Vietnamese in official meetings was symbolic rather than practical. It reminded young people of their Vietnamese cultural identity and heritage. Participants had come from many European cities, and even a letter of support from the Vietnamese youth organization in Tokyo was read to the audience.

The Vietnamese national anthem was played at the opening ceremony, while everyone in the room stood up. The president of the UJVF introduced all the officials, among them the general secretary of the Vietnamese consulate in Paris, who was the first to speak. He talked about the cooperation between the Vietnamese community and *mère patrie* (mother country) and congratulated the European-born Vietnamese on their work toward maintaining an alliance between overseas Vietnamese communities and Vietnam. He stressed that the French-born generation of the *Viet Kieu* (Vietnamese immigrants) were the future leaders of the organization. The president of the leadership committee of the UJVF addressed her remarks to the general secretary, reassuring him of the organization's commitment to the reconstruction of Vietnam. She also praised Vietnamese youth for their participation in the cultural and social activities in the UGVF community, i.e., sports, preparation for Tet, and tutoring Vietnamese high school students. She announced that following an opening ceremony, discussion sessions were going to be held in small groups. Included in the three sessions were such topics as "Information and Social Relations," "Cultural and Sports Activities," and "The High School Student Tutorial Program." I decided to participate in the first one, which was the most controversial. The discussion was led by three women, a twenty-four-year-old doctor, a twenty-two-year-old civil servant, and a twenty-seven-year-old pharmacist. Forty people attended the session. The participants expressed their frustration over the lack of information on the economics and politics of Vietnam. Then the discussion focused on the newspaper *Bulledingue,* which some people felt should not be censored by the UGVF, while others argued that it gave the UGVF a bad image, which could be used as propaganda by anticommunist organizations.

In the afternoon, at the general meeting, the president read the text of the 1984–1986 commitment and goals of the UJVF. As soon as she finished, Phuong stood up and said she was opposed to the use of the word *solidarity* in the text to describe the relationship between the UGVF and the UJVF. She argued that it implied that the UJVF was under the authority of the UGVF. Someone else in the audience replied that the UJVF was part of the UGVF and therefore it was important that the UJVF show its loyalty to the UGVF and follow its political line. The arguments went on for an hour between Phuong and other members of the audience until the UJVF president broke up the discussion and asked to proceed with the agenda. Phuong was not ready to give up. She said she also wanted to discuss the sentence that included the phrase "promoting a good relationship with Laos and Cambodia." Some people in the audience asked her to shut up. Everyone knew Phuong was considered to be a troublemaker. But Phuong went on, saying that it was more appropriate for the organization to promote a better relationship with France than with Laos and Cambodia. She argued that Laos and Cambodia were two countries very far away from the Vietnamese community in France. And she added that the sentence was once again part of the Hanoi political discourse that matched the interests of Hanoi rather than those of the overseas Vietnamese communities. When she asked participants to vote on the issue, they refused. One young Vietnamese woman who was getting upset by the whole discussion told her that when one joined the UGVF, one should agree with its politics and that this was a matter of principle. The president postponed discussion on the topic for the day and went on to the original agenda of the meeting. The next day she announced that while the word *solidarity* was still going to be used, the controversial sentence would be changed to "better relations with Laos, Cambodia, and France." After dinner there was evening entertainment presented by the UJVF, a traditional Vietnamese dance performed by young French-born Vietnamese and a comedy. The comedy was a satire on the problems of the French-born Vietnamese in the UGVF. Phuong was the central character. During the play, I was sitting next to Phuong and she herself laughed at the jokes they made about her.

The next day, the report of each session was presented to the general meeting. The president reminded UJVF participants of their role in giving financial and intellectual support to Vietnam. The closing ceremony was followed by the election of a new UJVF leadership committee for the next two years. Another woman, a thirty-year-old doctor, was elected president of the organization.

While the organization is redefining the goals and purposes of the Parisian Vietnamese community, changes are inevitable. Although the pre-1975 Vietnamese have said that they want to return to Vietnam, it is likely that after twenty years, most of them will remain in France. The French-born Vietnamese are challenging the UGVF leaders by demanding that their community have more political autonomy from Hanoi. In spite of internal conflicts and changes, however, the UGVF members are not likely to leave the organization to join the anticommunist organizations.

Chapter 6
The Anticommunist Faction

Unlike the pro-Hanoi faction, the anticommunist faction is not represented by a single political organization. Instead, it includes a set of social and political networks equivalent to that of the UGVF. All the anticommunist organizations are bound to each other by a single political ideology, the overthrow of the Vietnamese Communist party and the establishment of a democracy in Vietnam. While the UGVF leaders refuse to acknowledge the importance of factionalism in the Vietnamese community, the leaders of anticommunist organizations actively promote political division within the community. Indeed, they encourage immigrants and refugees to join either of the two factions. One informant, a forty-five-year-old leader, made a clear distinction between "them" (the communists), referring to the UGVF members, and "us" (the anticommunist political organizations).

In their political discourse, the UGVF leaders no longer use the concept of factionalism in reference to politics in the Vietnamese community, but instead emphasize solidarity. In contrast, the anticommunist leaders openly base their political discourse on the factional split of the community.

Before 1975, no strongly centralized anticommunist political network existed. The large number of anticommunist political groups in Paris corresponded to the numerous scattered political parties existing in South Vietnam. They all shared a common cause, however: opposition to the reunification of the two Vietnams. At that time, they were a minority group within the Vietnamese community, so they kept a low profile. In contrast, the UGVF was actively mobilizing the long-established Vietnamese community around the antiwar issue.

In 1975, the sudden influx of Vietnamese refugees shifted the balance of power between the two factions. The anticommunist political organizations grew rapidly over the next ten years. To compete effectively with the UGVF for the loyalty of the new immigrants, they attempted to coordinate their splinter groups and build a unified organization.

The Anticommunist Organizations

For the purpose of this study, I classify the anticommunist groups into three main categories—student, leadership, and social and cultural organizations.

The student organizations are what I call "cover-up organizations," meaning that the students are the ones who make public appearances. When I first entered the anticommunist political networks, I was easily able to contact the leaders of the student organizations whereas it took many months to make contact with members of the leadership organizations. The student organizations hold social and cultural events, organize demonstrations, and recruit new members. They also organize meetings with other Vietnamese student organizations from Vietnamese communities established in other French cities and other European countries. In Paris there are two main student organizations: L'Amicale des Vietnamiens de la Région de Paris-Sud (The Friendship Association of the Vietnamese of South Paris), and L'Association Générale des Etudiants Vietnamiens de Paris (The Association of the Vietnamese Students of Paris). They both originated in universities. Today their leadership consists of students and former students. They use social and cultural activities as a device to recruit new members and enhance their financial support. Both of these organizations participate in political meetings with the leadership organization, to which I was never invited.

I met Bui, a twenty-seven-year-old man in the anticommunist political network, through a leader of L'Amicale des Vietnamiens de la Région de Paris-Sud at their Tet event in February 1984. Upon my arrival in Paris, I had a few contacts in the UGVF through a French scholar, but I had none at all in the anticommunist network. After a long discussion, Bui said he would let me know if he could talk to me further after checking with his colleagues. Knowing that I had been working with the UGVF, the leaders of anticommunist organizations feared that I was also a communist spying on their political activities. He called me up a few weeks after the Tet to announce that he would be able to participate in an interview. Bui became one of my best informants in the anticommunist networks. He understood the purpose of my research and was willing to help me become integrated in the anticommunist political network. Although Bui was open in giving me information about his political organization and letting me know when there was a social or cultural gathering, he refused to help me make contact with the leadership political organizations because he lacked the authority to do so. He introduced me exclusively to members of L'Amicale des Vietnamiens de la Région de Paris-Sud, people of his own generation. In order to extend my own network to other organizations, I had to introduce myself through people I met at social gatherings.

The purpose of L'Amicale des Vietnamiens de la Région de Paris-Sud is to organize cultural activities like theater and traditional dances. Its headquarters is located in a suburban town southwest of Paris. Because its activities cannot be staged without plenty of active participation by members, recruitment is essential to the group. Men and women from the age of sixteen to thirty-five are recruited to write scripts, make costumes, and otherwise help put on the performances. These performances are a year-round activity and members work weekends and evenings to ensure their success. Other anticommunist organizations however, such as L'Association Générale des Etudiants Vietnamiens de Paris and L'Alliance Vietnamienne, manned the surrounding booths to distribute political pamphlets and flyers to the French.

L'Association Générale des Etudiants Vietnamiens de Paris was created in 1964, much earlier than L'Amicale des Vietnamiens de la Région de Paris-Sud. Anh, a twenty-five-year-old member of the latter organization, explained to me that in the past the two were rivals, competing with each other for new members. But in the past few years, they have worked together to coordinate their efforts for organizing demonstrations and cultural events. L'Association Générale des Etudiants Vietnamiens de Paris has its headquarters in the thirteenth arrondissement. It offers a variety of sports activities such as volleyball, football, and tennis. In Paris the organization was given access to a recreational facility in the thirteenth arrondissement by Mayor Chirac, who became prime minister in 1986 and who represents France's Conservative party in Mitterand's coalition government.

The association publishes a monthly newspaper, *Nhan Ban,* written in Vietnamese. Since *Nhan Ban* is a political newspaper, Vietnamese-owned stores refused to carry it, with the exception of "Orient," a Vietnamese grocery store in the fifteenth arrondissement. *Nhan Ban* focuses on political activities of the anticommunist organizations. It also supplies reports on the "freedom fighters" in Vietnam. Like *DoanKet,* the UGVF newspaper, *Nhan Ban* is primarily sent to the organization's membership. Recruitment of members is not so essential to the organization. Nam, an editor of *Nhan Ban,* told me that they primarily solicit financial contributions rather than members. The money is used to fund the anticommunist network, which publishes materials, rents space for meetings, and organizes social events.

Just as the UGVF members meet on a daily basis at the "Foyer des Etudiants Vietnamiens" in the fifteenth, members of its counterpart anticommunist organizations take their meals together at a restaurant in the thirteenth. The restaurant is located near the headquarters of L'Association Générale des Etudiants Vietnamiens de Paris. It is especially patronized by students and single men. They do not eat at reserved tables but walk in and join friends already seated. I was told that it was a place where one did not go to eat alone, but to see friends.

Tuan, a twenty-five-year-old computer engineer, had invited me to join him for lunch one day. I expected to have lunch in a restaurant near his job in the twelfth arrondissement, but instead he suggested that we eat in the thirteenth to see everyone else. Because of the traffic, it was a long drive before we got to the restaurant. I was astounded when Tuan told me that he made this trip every day. Obviously this restaurant was an important center of his social and political life. When we arrived at the restaurant, many of my informants in the anticommunist political network were already there eating. Tuan was utterly at home, greeting everyone and making jokes before we finally sat down to eat. The dishes served were only Vietnamese, and, as in other restaurants in the area, were cheap. One could buy a bowl of soup, *pho*, for only three dollars.

In contrast to the student organizations, the "leadership organizations" operate "behind the scenes." They are mostly composed of former South Vietnamese leaders and intellectuals. These organizations, Le Conseil Mondial des Communautés Vietnamiennes (International Council of Vietnamese Communities) and L'Union des Vietnamiens Libres d'Outre-Mer (The Association of the Free Overseas Vietnamese), were created in the early 1980s. They coordinate all Vietnamese anticommunist organizations worldwide. Their leaders' goal is to overthrow the regime of Hanoi and set up a new democratic government. The creation of a Vietnamese government in exile has been one of the most difficult tasks of these organizations. Manh, a former leader of one such organization, explained to me how factionalism within the Vietnamese anticommunist movement has prevented it from establishing a united front. Although all the organizations are "anticommunist" or against Hanoi, they cannot agree on the type of government that would replace the existing Vietnamese Communist party. For example, most of the South Vietnamese military leaders fled to the United States. They naturally filled leadership posts in the overseas anticommunist organizations. Their concept of the type of government an anticommunist victory would bring, however, is quite different from the vision of their nonmilitary counterparts in Vietnamese organizations in France. The Vietnamese anticommunist leaders in the United States favor replacing the Hanoi government with a military regime. The Vietnamese anticommunist organizations in France, however, strongly support a democratic government.

Since I had only a few informants in these organizations, I found it especially difficult to establish contacts at the leadership level. A former leader of one these organizations had given me other leaders' phone numbers along with a brief summary of their activities. He had asked me not to give his name away when I called these people for an interview and to pretend I had gotten their names through a French governmental office. Upon my first call I realized that it was a big mistake. People could not understand why I was calling them and how I had gotten their names.

I presented my lie, but understandably they did not believe me. Out of the six names I was given, only two of the people agreed, reluctantly, to meet me. This was after an hour-long phone call of solicitation on my part.

These organizations are very elitist in regard to membership. I was told by a member of these organizations that the leadership organizations recruit Vietnamese intellectuals, mostly within the refugee community. Le Conseil Mondial des Communautés Vietnamiennes, for instance, is composed of only 130 active members. The organization publishes newsletters and monthly newspapers and distributes them only to members. I was unable to obtain copies.

Besides these major organizations, there are a number of less significant political ones. Usually they are led by one person and supported by only a few followers. Some of the splinter organizations have as few as fifteen members. They work independently from the larger associations and are seen by the Vietnamese as unconnected. They are, however, politically allied with the anticommunist groups, and participate in collective fund-raising and demonstrations. L'Association Des Amis de Que Me (Association of the Friends of Que Me) is one of the best examples of a splinter association. Over the last ten years, the organization has been subject to strong criticism from Vietnamese immigrants. The leader, Nam, has been involved in highly questionable fund-raising activities. In 1976, Nam launched an urgent fund-raising campaign to finance a ship to rescue the Vietnamese boat people. Even though the campaign was very successful, the ship never left Europe. An officer at a French refugee agency told me that the donors were victims of fraud, but there has not been any solid evidence of this. The Vietnamese consider this organization a disgrace to the community.

Social Support Organizations

Social organizations such as L'Association d'Entre-Aide des Vietnamiens Agés d'Outre-Mer (Mutual Association for the Overseas Vietnamese Elderly), Hanh Dong (L'Organisation d'Entre-Aide des Réfugiés [Organization of Mutual Assistance for the

Refugees]), Khanh Anh (Association Bouddhique Vietnamienne in Bagneux [The Buddhist Vietnamese Association in Bagneux]), Le Village Vietnamien (The Vietnamese Village), Le Centre Culturel Vietnamien (The Vietnamese Cultural Center) at APARASE (Association Parisienne aux Réfugiés de l'Asie du Sud-Est [The Parisian Association for Southeast Asian Refugees]), La Mission Catholique (the Catholic Mission), and Les Scouts Vietnamiens (The Vietnamese Scout Organization) are not involved directly in political activities, but they still belong to the anticommunist political network. They act primarily as social support groups whose goal is to help refugees adapt to French society. Even though they are primarily social organizations, their membership tends to be restricted to anticommunist supporters. This means that some Vietnamese with divergent political opinions feel excluded. For example, Van, a seventy-five-year-old man, explained that the Association d'Entre-Aide des Vietnamiens Agés d'Outre-Mer in the fifteenth arrondissement has strong ties with anticommunist organizations. "Because I do not share the same political views," he said, "I am not welcome in there." "It is a shame for a man of my age," he added, "not to be able to participate in a Vietnamese social organization for older people."

At APARASE, the cultural center for refugees, the Vietnamese workers do not hide their political affiliations with anticommunist organizations. The center is ostensibly a nonpolitical French organization whose goal is to serve the Asian immigrant population in Paris. The center opened in March 1984 and was sponsored by Mayor Chirac of Paris. APARASE offers cultural activities, such as photography, painting, and sports, and social services, such as literacy classes for Vietnamese refugees who do not read or write in their own language, French classes for Southeast Asian refugees, and tutoring for Vietnamese high school students. The classes are taught by both French and Asian volunteers. I discovered that the Vietnamese people who worked there were all members of anticommunist political organizations. Although the center is nonpolitical, the selection of Vietnamese membership is done by the Vietnamese themselves. A Vietnamese manager told me that he was concerned with communist infiltration in the center (meaning the UGVF). He said that "they come and try to gather information about the refugees who come to the center, but we can always spot them, because they cannot pass for refugees, and we kick them out."

L'Organisation d'Entre-Aide des Réfugiés, created in 1977 to assist refugees, is another social institution that tries to ease the culture shock experienced by the refugees. This organization publishes Vietnamese books and distributes them freely among refugees. It is a small enterprise financed by private French and Vietnamese donations and run by a small group of young Vietnamese refugees. I got in contact with the organization through one of my informants who was a member of an anticommunist organization. After talking to Anh, a thirty-year-old leader, I was invited to have an interview with him one November evening. I knew that L'Organisation d'Entre-Aide des Réfugiés was an underground organization, so I had expected to visit him at his apartment rather than at the organization headquarters, a small two-room rented apartment with a printing machine and stacks of papers and written materials. I was welcomed by other members of the organization who had been invited by Anh to participate in the interview. They invited me to sit down at the only table in the room, and they offered me tea and cookies. Most of them were students or former students with the exception of one, a thirty-year-old refugee who helped with the printing machine. He had been in France for four years and yet did not speak any French. He explained that there were many other Vietnamese like him who did not need to speak French. They worked in Vietnamese businesses and had little contact with the French. Half an hour later, Anh arrived and we all talked about the role of the organization. Manh claimed that the organization was linked to other anticommunist organizations but he refused to give me their names. They showed me the books they were printing. Like all the written material they distribute, these contained strong political statements about Vietnam. Even their book on learning the French language had a political statement inserted at the bottom of every other page. Such slogans as "Vietnam can be freed from communism if we keep on fighting" were interspersed with grammar and syntax. Manh explained that it was important to remind the refugees of their duties toward their country. Everyone involved volunteered their time and expertise to write, publish, and distribute materials to the refugees. The organization subsisted on donations from the larger Vietnamese organizations.

Khanh Anh, the Buddhist temple at Bagneux, a southwest suburb of Paris, is reputed to be the most political of the religious organizations. I visited the temple one Sunday afternoon in late September. I had made my first contact with Hai, a twenty-four-year-old member, at the "Children's Festival" and then was invited to go visit the temple. From the outside, the temple looks like any other suburban house in Bagneux. If it had not been for the nameplate on the wall, I would not have been able to differentiate it from any other house. I was keen to visit the temple because I had been told that the monks were extremely political. I had seen them participating in anticommunist demonstrations and making political speeches. I had previously tried to interview the principal monk of the temple but without much success.

I entered the temple from the back door of a house that led into a remodeled basement containing a large kitchen and dining room. My first reaction was to compare Khan Anh to the Truc Lam temple. Whereas the building of Truc Lam is grandiose and therefore conspicuous in the neighborhood, the discreet appearance of the Khan Anh temple seemed to indicate the poverty of its followers. I was also surprised to see so many young refugee men in their early twenties, when ordinarily it is the elderly people, mostly women, who worship on Sunday. The youths I saw did not, however, participate in any religious rituals. I was told later by Manh that those are the young men training to become monks. He explained that Khan Anh is one of the few temples that takes novices. Since I arrived at lunchtime, I was invited to join people sitting at large tables for a vegetarian meal. Whereas at the Truc Lam my visits did not seem to disturb the members, since I was very often mistaken for a first-generation Eurasian, at Khanh Anh people knew I was not Vietnamese. They were friendly and curious about my visit. The elderly women were refugees from South Vietnam. They came to the temple every Sunday to pray and socialize. Our discussion was suddenly interrupted by a voice from a loudspeaker above our heads asking the worshippers to join the monks in the ceremony hall for a prayer. As we went up the stairs, I noticed that loudspeakers were in all the rooms of the building. The prayers were then available to anyone who was in the building. I could even hear them in the bathroom I used before joining the worshippers.

On the second floor was a large ceremony room with a big Buddha at the center. On the walls on both sides of the Buddha were pictures of people whom I believe were deceased members of the congregation. All the worshippers, mostly older women and a few older men, were kneeling on the carpeted floor with large Buddhist prayer books on small stands placed in front of them. For the two hours I was there everyone read the prayers aloud, led by a monk.

For me, this service was memorable, dramatizing the potential discomforts in participant observation. I was not used to kneeling for that long, and my legs became numb. I could not leave because I was caught between two women with whom I shared a book, and I was the one in charge of turning the pages. Never did I have a chance to look around the room. I had to keep up with the prayers, and my neighbor, an older woman, would jab my elbow when I was reading the wrong line. I kept contemplating the numbers of pages in the fat book that we still had to cover before reaching the end. After two hours I decided that regardless of whether it was rude, I would politely excuse myself, saying I would be back. When I left the room, the ceremony was still going on. I went into the conference room where I chatted with a handful of young refugee men while waiting to interview the worshippers after the prayers. Unfortunately, when the prayers finally ended, everyone left the temple very quickly. On this late winter Sunday afternoon, it was indeed already starting to get dark outside.

Les Scouts Vietnamiens is another social organization that is actually part of the anticommunist political network. The movement was founded in 1979 by former Vietnamese scouts who had come to France as refugees. In 1984, there were approximately one hundred Vietnamese scouts, whose ages ranged from seven to thirty. The young scouts are primarily children of middle-class Vietnamese refugees from South Vietnam. The goal of the Scouts is to reinforce Vietnamese cultural identity among young people. In 1984, the Scouts were the only organization that dealt with the young French-born Vietnamese. It was a shock for me to meet scout leaders older than twenty-five because in French scouting organizations, the leaders are twenty-five or younger. Most scouts are Buddhists but a few are Catholics. Modeled after the South Vietnamese Scouts, the group is officially part of the Scouts de France but has retained its own uniforms and traditions. I was told that similar Vietnamese Scout organizations have been formed elsewhere in Europe, the United States, Canada, and Australia.

I was invited to visit the scout headquarters after meeting some scouts at the Tet, where they had a booth. They were very friendly. A couple of young girls asked me if I was going to join them. I had to explain that I had passed the age but had been a scout myself in the past. Nga, a twenty-seven-year-old scout leader, told me that Vietnamese is the only language spoken in the group and that the games they learn are Vietnamese. She explained that Vietnamese children raised in France did not have any opportunity to use their native language outside of the family and in a social group. While Nga was talking to me in the main hall, young children in uniforms were playing Vietnamese games. Nga asked me if I wanted to join a patrol meeting held in a smaller room. They were deciding on who was going to be the chief of the patrol. One of them, a thirteen-year-old girl, said that she wanted to be the chief. But she was rejected by the group on the grounds that her Vietnamese was not good enough. I was told that the big event, as for any other Scout organization, was a month-long camping trip in the summer. The young girls confided that that was the fun part of being a scout. As one put it, this was a chance to be in the wilderness with her friends away from the city and her parents.

One of my informants, Mai, told me that even though the Scouts is a nonpolitical organization, most of its leaders are supportive members of anticommunist organizations. The scouts also help in any social events sponsored by these anticommunist organizations. For example, in 1984 they participated in the celebration of Buddha's birthday, an event organized by Khan Anh and other Buddhist organizations. They distributed programs at the door and helped people find places to sit. Though scout leaders participate in anticommunist demonstrations, they do not wear their uniforms.

La Mission Catholique in the fourteenth arrondissement is yet another nonpolitical organization, run by Vietnamese priests and nuns and dependent on the diocese of Paris. The mission is located in a large building with space for meetings, masses, class-rooms, priests' and nuns' offices, and a big kitchen. I frequently visited the mission because I was welcome there. Sister Ann was al-ways trying to recruit me to teach a French class. I had once agreed to act as a substitute teacher, but I refused to do it on a daily basis. A primary function of the mission is to help refugees adjust to French society by teaching them the French language and offering them small jobs. Many refugees who have just arrived spend a great deal of their time at the mission. They go there daily to learn French, to get advice, and to find a job. The mission offers Viet-namese refugees a place to socialize and find moral support. Every Sunday there were masses. The nuns and some French volunteers would take the refugees for a tour of Paris. The refugees were not all Catholics. I met a number of them who were Buddhists but used the mission for its social services. The head nun was Sister Marie, a forty-five-year-old woman who tried to find jobs for the refugees by contacting possible employers and setting up interviews. She ex-plained that it was very important for the refugees to become self-sufficient by learning French and finding employment.

Sister Marie claimed that the mission was not political. How-ever, the outer walls of the mission were covered with political posters, reminding us that even the mission was the target of politi-cal fights in the community. In an interview with Father Pierre, I learned that a few years earlier, the mission had been a bat-tleground of political conflict between two priests. Eventually Fa-ther Michel and his supporters left the mission and formed their own congregation. According to Father Pierre, they were mem-bers of the UGVF.

Today there are about sixty Vietnamese priests in France; in Vietnam there are two hundred, many of whom are in reeducation camps. Father Pierre pointed out that young Vietnamese men who wanted to become priests had to escape from Vietnam to get their training. In France, only twenty of them worked with the Catholic Mission, while the others worked in French churches. But he pointed out that all the Vietnamese priests meet four times a year for moral support. He no longer has contact with the Catholic progressive group.

Among the French organizations allied with the anticommunist faction is L'Institut de l'Asie du Sud-Est (The Institute of Southeast Asia), sponsored by Le Ministère de la Solidarité et de l'Action Sociale (The Ministry of Solidarity and Social Action) and the Sorbonne. Before 1975, the Institute was a dormitory exclusively for South Vietnamese students who had come to Paris in order to pursue their studies with a scholarship from the French government. But after the fall of Saigon, the center lost its purpose, and today it is a dormitory for foreign students from other countries. The Institute, however, still offers classes to prepare Vietnamese high school students for their high school diplomas. These students, whose ages range from thirteen to eighteen, are children of Vietnamese refugees. Although Vietnamese is their first language, they neither read nor write it. The classes, therefore, are aimed at preparing them to take Vietnamese as a second language for the high school examination (the Baccalauréat). The classes are offered once a week for two hours on Wednesday afternoons when the students are not attending their high schools in Paris. There are three classes, for first-, second-, and third-level students, taught by Vietnamese teachers who used to teach Vietnamese in high schools in Vietnam.

I had enrolled for one semester in one of these classes at the second level. There were about twenty middle-class students attending the class. They were all diligent students who took great interest in the class. The textbook used was provided by the Institute. In fact, the Institute is also publishing books written in Vietnamese for the Vietnamese community. The director of the Institute, a French scholar in his fifties, pointed out that most Vietnamese books are written by Vietnamese communist scholars. He told me that it was important to publish Vietnamese materials that were not politically oriented. He said that the books were mostly reprinted from Vietnamese books, novels, and poems that he had collected in Vietnam. These books were then sold in French bookstores like "FNAC" (one of the largest bookstores in Paris). He told me that he was himself strongly opposed to communism, but refused to give me any more information about the links between the Institute and Vietnamese anticommunist organizations. He just mentioned to me that he occasionally meets with leaders of Vietnamese anticommunist organizations.

The Role of Anticommunist Organizations

Political Activities

In contrast with the leaders of the UGVF, whose goal is to create an overseas Vietnamese community, leaders and members of the anticommunist organizations claim that the Vietnamese refugees' resettlement in France is only temporary. Although many refugees have taken French citizenship, they still consider themselves "political refugees" whose political loyalty remains with Vietnam rather than France.

The anticommunist organizations' political discourse reveals that they are planning to take action against the communist regime in Hanoi. Their goals are: (1) to compete with the communist organization for power within the Vietnamese community; (2) to form a new government to take over the leadership of Vietnam after the defeat of the communists; (3) to support the "freedom fighters" in Vietnam in their efforts to overthrow the communists; and (4) to ally themselves with non-Vietnamese anticommunist organizations to gain support from the international community.

The anticommunists insist on having two social and political communities. They want the French to know that the UGVF does not represent the Vietnamese community, and they force the Vietnamese to ally themselves with one faction or the other. Anticommunist leaders believe that building a separate community challenges the power of the UGVF. On the one hand, the leaders of the UGVF claim that there are not two Vietnamese communities and that their opposition, if any, is extremely weak. On the other hand, the anticommunists claim that the UGVF directs much of its energy toward eliminating the opposition. Van, a leader of an anticommunist organization, told me that the UGVF infiltrates their political organizations and stages conflicts among political groups. Van blames the UGVF for the lack of unity among the anticommunists.

Despite the claims of the UGVF, the presence of two Vietnamese communities in Paris is readily apparent. Anticommunist political activities are far from invisible. A few months before their Tet celebration, for instance, members of the UGVF publicized the event by lining the streets with posters. They advertised primarily in arrondissements where there is a high concentration of Vietnamese (the fifth, thirteenth, and fifteenth). A few days later, these same posters were covered with anticommunist propaganda.

"Viet cong"; "Cuong-quyet tay-chay Tet Viet cong"; "De quoc moi cong-san So-Viet Nga cut Khoi Viet-Nam"; "Nhung ten Viet-gian cong-san hai nguoi con chut liem-si hay tro ve Ha-noi lam toi to cho bon ac-quy Duan Dong Chinh Tho."[1]

The campaign against UGVF's social and cultural events was for the benefit of recent refugees who might not have been aware of their communist sponsorship. I have not seen any fighting between members of the two factions, but I was told that a few years earlier confrontations were common. The anticommunist leaders would have a demonstration in any place where the UGVF organized a social or cultural event, and, according to my informants, it would always turn into a fight between the two groups.

Demonstrations are another means used by the anticommunists to establish their political strength in France. For example, every year in April all Vietnamese anticommunist organizations participate in a demonstration against the fall of Saigon in 1975. In 1984, the demonstration consisted of a march from the Trocadero to the Soviet consulate. That year, the target of the demonstration was the Soviets. Early Saturday afternoon, a thousand Vietnamese gathered at the Trocadero, a large beautiful plaza with the Eiffel Tower in the background. While we were waiting for people to arrive, a car with a loudspeaker parked in front of the plaza and played the South Vietnamese anthem. Among the Vietnamese refugees were French supporters of the worldwide anticommunist movement, French veterans of the Indochina war, and extreme right-wing party members trying to recruit Vietnamese refugees and anticommunist Afghan leaders. Among the Vietnamese leadership were a delegation of six monks

---

1. "Communists"; "Resolutely boycott the Communist Tet"; "Imperialist Communist Soviets get out of Vietnam"; "If you Vietnamese communist traitors still have any sense of decency go back to Hanoi as lackeys of the monsters Duan, Dong, Chinh and Tho."

from the Khanh Anh temple and leaders of the anticommunist Vietnamese political organizations. After a speech by the Vietnamese leaders, an Afghan leader gave a talk condemning the Vietnamese communists and the Soviet invasions of Third World countries. In front of the speakers a giant South Vietnamese flag was held by six teenagers in blue uniforms (jeans and blue shirts). We were each given a sheet of paper on which slogans were printed in Vietnamese and French. After the speeches, the march started, with the car bearing the loudspeaker at its head; the loudspeaker was used to direct the crowd and lead the chants. I marched with one of my informants, Anh, a twenty-three-year-old engineering student who was also a Vietnamese scout. He gave me the sheet of slogans and like everyone else I chanted.

This was a peaceful march that drew the support of approximately one thousand refugees. They chanted slogans such as "Soviets out of Vietnam," "Down with the Soviets," and "Vietnamese communists are killers." The march ran through the sixteenth arrondissement, an upper-class French neighborhood, where demonstrations seldom take place. It was a quiet Saturday afternoon. Very few people showed up on the sidewalks, though a few peered out of windows to see what was happening. We were stopped a block away from the Soviet consulate by a barricade erected by the French police. With the Soviet consulate in the background, more speeches were given. Later on that evening, a meeting was organized at the Palais de la Mutualité in the fifth arrondissement. Only one of the largest rooms upstairs was opened. At the entrance was a donation box. Anh was solicited by an older Vietnamese man who reminded him that he was making enough money to contribute to the cause. Anh was at first reluctant, but finally put a bill in the box. There was a very casual atmosphere, with children running around and people chatting in all parts of the room. Despite this pleasant ambience, I found that there was an obvious social distance between the leaders and members of the organizations and the supportive refugees who came to participate. Most leaders and members were men dressed in suits. They mingled together talking politics, while the refugees, composed of families in modest clothes, kept to themselves in another part of the room. I had always been amazed by the amount of Vietnamese food one could purchase at UGVF social events. In contrast, at anticommunist events like this one, there were only sandwiches, cokes, and Vietnamese cake.

For the first few hours people chatted with members of their own social network, while a Vietnamese band played in the background. Then a choir of young Vietnamese went on stage and sang the Vietnamese anthem. This was followed by a political discussion about the situation in Vietnam. The speakers condemned Soviet intervention in Vietnam, Laos, and Cambodia and proposed a coalition with refugees from Laos and Cambodia to fight communism. They also proposed that the Vietnamese ally themselves with refugees from other countries who had fled communism. Then they gave a brief history of Vietnam to remind the audience that Vietnam had always fought foreign domination and that it was again time for the people to unite and free their country. Hanoi was portrayed not as an independent communist government, but rather as a puppet of the USSR, like Angola and Afghanistan. They ended by discussing the problems of the boat people and Thai piracy and telling the audience horrifying stories of boat people's experiences en route to freedom. After the talk, a dance was organized that lasted until the next morning. I did not stay for the dance because I was too exhausted from the tiring afternoon march.

On another occasion, the student political organizations organized a demonstration in front of the French national TV station to protest against the television series entitled "Vietnam" written by a French-American journalist team and directed in France by Henri Turenne. The protestors claimed that the movie was biased and that the Vietnamese communists were portrayed as heroes. They felt that the French public was being deceived by the movie's one-sided approach to the war. They requested television time to discuss the movie with its director Turenne and formed a picket line in front of the TV station to enforce their demands. I was unable to observe the demonstration, because at that time I had no contacts in the anticommunist network. Later I saw a videotape of the demonstration at a social gathering after the Tet celebration of L'Amicale des Vietnamiens de la Région Paris-Sud. The videotape was shown to the members and everyone commented on the footage covering the demonstration and laughed at everyone else who had been there.

After numerous letters of protest to President Mitterand, their request for television time was finally granted. One of my informants, Dr. Nguyen, a forty-five-year-old refugee and former South Vietnamese military officer, told me that all the organizations had to put a lot of pressure on the French government, using all their French rightist political connections to win their demands. They were eventually given only fifteen minutes at the end of the series for a discussion with Mr. Turenne. According to Dr. Nguyen, it was nevertheless a victory because it was a way to let the French public know that Vietnamese anticommunist organizations existed in France. I, however, do not think that this discussion had much impact on the French public. Instead they adopted Mr. Turenne's point of view. Mr. Turenne did not deny the political bias of the movie, but argued that the film had merit because it contained documentary footage supplied by Hanoi that had never previously been made available to the French public.

I found that Vietnamese history is another issue of contention between leaders of the two factions. Pro-Hanoi leaders claim that the Communist party was the main political force that fought colonialism and later freed Vietnam from foreign domination. The anticommunist leaders argue that the Vietnamese Communist party was armed and backed by the Chinese Communist party and gained power in Vietnam by using military force and intimidating the population. Hai, a forty-year-old leader of a student organization, explained that before 1945, there were many nationalist Vietnamese organizations that opposed French colonialism but refused to join the communists. He felt that "they may not have been as united as the communist organizations but they played as important a role in the independence of Vietnam as the communists did." He reported that in South Vietnam, many Vietnamese political organizations were also opposed to Diem and the military junta, but knew better than to ally themselves with the Communist party. He added that "the communists committed a lot of atrocities in Vietnam but the movie did not focus on that side of the story." Another informant, Bui, told me that the anticommunist leadership recognized the mistakes and weaknesses of the former South Vietnamese government and the corrupt society it created. He pointed out that the Vietnamese Communist party is a totalitarian regime that has not given the country a democratic government.

To support the Vietnamese "freedom fighters" is to support the counter-revolution struggling to free Vietnam from communism. Not all of the organizations officially admit to providing such support. Instead they funnel financial support through the more radical underground organizations. At all social and cultural events, members are asked to make contributions for the benefit of "freedom fighters" in Vietnam.

In 1984, the French government targeted the organization L'Association Générale des Etudiants Vietnamiens de Paris for an investigation of its fund-raising during a Tet celebration. I was told by a French officer at the Préfecture de Police in Paris that this organization was involved in illegal fund-raising. According to the 1910 French law, an "association," i.e., a nonprofit organization, cannot practice fund-raising for political purposes. The group's association license was suspended for several months during the investigation.

In addition to fund-raising, some organizations recruit "freedom fighters" in Paris. I was given the name and phone number of Tro, a sixty-five-year-old leader of one of these political organizations, by an informant who was a former leader of another Vietnamese political organization. My informant asked me not to mention his name. When I first called Tro over the phone, I was unable to tell him the name of the contact. Instead I followed instructions and told him that I got his name through my own connections in the French government. Tro suspected the lie and was suspicious of my research. We had a long discussion on the phone before he finally agreed to see me a few weeks later.

I met him at his headquarters in Paris in a small ground-floor apartment. I was received by two young Vietnamese men in their early twenties who did not speak much French. After explaining to them the nature of my visit, I was finally invited to go in. There were three rooms: a conference room, a dining room, and a kitchen in the back. I was very surprised at the luxurious furniture in the conference room. A large wooden table stood in the center of the room, surrounded by black and red chairs. The walls were austere, bearing only a South Vietnamese flag and a few pictures of Vietnam. After offering me a cup of tea and a seat, the young men cross-examined me regarding the purpose of my visit. During this discussion I learned that both of them were refugees who had been in France for only a few months. They told me about their desire to return to Vietnam to fight communism.

When Tro arrived with two other men, my two companions rapidly adjourned to the kitchen. Tro invited me to sit down at the dinner table. It was a difficult interview, because Tro was not ready to give me much information about his organization. He answered some of my questions, but refused to answer those he disliked. He gave me a copy of his curriculum vitae that he had brought with him and advised me to consult it carefully. I learned that Tro was now sixty-five. He had been a pharmacist in Saigon and had started to get involved in politics as early as 1926. He first participated in the anticolonialist movement in Paris, where he was a student, and later participated in the peace movement in Vietnam after he returned there to work. He fled Vietnam with his family after the fall of Saigon in 1975. Tro also showed me a picture of himself in front of the Palais des Congrès in Geneva during a hunger strike in 1979 protesting the situation of the "boat people." He informed me that he was now recruiting young refugee men in "Foyers d'Hébergement" (refugee centers) to go back and fight communism. These were young men who arrived without relatives and did not want to stay in France. Feeling lonely, they only wanted to go back to Vietnam. Tro refused to tell me who was financing their return, to which country they were being sent, and from which countries they were leaving. He was annoyed with my questions and decided after an hour that the interview was over.

This interview illustrates the problems of doing research on a politically sensitive issue. People did not always trust me, because I was often mistaken for a communist spy. I was, for instance, seldom invited to visit the headquarters of the anticommunist organization because the leaders were extremely suspicious of the kind of research I was doing. One of my informants once almost cancelled a dinner invitation because he was not sure it was appropriate to have me in his apartment while he was working on making signs for a demonstration. No informants told me everything they knew. I often had to cross-check information by confronting all of my former informants and questioning new informants on the same issues.

Social Activities

One of the most important events of the year is the Tet celebration, for which L'Amicale des Vietnamiens de la Région de Paris-Sud provides the entertainment. For communist and anticommunist organizations alike, the Tet celebration is an opportunity to make a political statement in both the Vietnamese and the French communities. Anh, a twenty-five-year-old, explained that for anticommunists, the Tet celebration was a way to let Vietnamese refugees know that they should not give up their battle against communism and should keep on supporting anticommunist organizations. The celebration was also a way of letting the French people know that the Vietnamese community was politically divided between communists and anticommunists.

Like the UGVF's Tet, that of L'Amicale des Vietnamiens de la Région Paris-Sud requires preparation starting six months in advance. Every year their Tet took place one week after the UGVF's. In 1984, the Tet was held for the first time at the Palais de la Mutualité in the fifth arrondissement. Tuan, a twenty-five-year-old member of L'Amicale des Vietnamiens de la Région de Paris-Sud, pointed out that the Palais de la Mutualité was very expensive to rent and it was only in 1984 that the organization was able to raise enough money to rent it.

In the hallways, booths were set up for various social organizations allied with such anticommunist organizations as the Scouts. Although the decorations were less grandiose than those of the UGVF's Tet, the display of the South Vietnamese flag in all rooms gave a political overtone to the decor. The walls of the auditorium, for instance, were covered with yellow-and-red-striped flags of the former South Vietnamese government. The crowd was one-third smaller and also less sophisticated than the one at the UGVF's Tet event. All of them were refugees, and though they had put on their best clothes for the occasion, they still looked like people who were not well off. Vietnamese was not only the official language of the show but also the language spoken by everyone (whereas French was the primary language at the UGVF's Tet event). The political nature of the event was unmistakable. The program started with a political speech reminding the audience that they all had to unite and keep on fighting against communist aggression in Vietnam and all over the world. Then there was a speech about the "freedom fighters" in Vietnam who were said to be building a resistance force. Even though the show had traditional dances, most of the entertainment was also extremely political. The plays were satires of life under the communists in Vietnam and strongly criticized Hanoi. One of the plays was called *Vietnamese Heaven under Communism* and illustrated the stupidity of the communist cadres. Everyone in the audience was laughing and seemed to appreciate this kind of humor.

A few weeks following the Tet, I was invited by Bui to participate in a party given by L'Amicale des Vietnamiens de la Région Paris-Sud on a Saturday night in the "salle des fêtes" of a small town in the suburbs of Paris. It was a post-Tet celebration for all the actors who had participated in the show. This was a small party for about fifty people, mostly young people in their twenties. They put on another small show for the audience, presenting all the slips that the actors had made during the show but no one in the audience had caught. In addition they reversed their roles. The men played the women and the women played the men. It was very funny and everyone was laughing hysterically.

Bui commented that everyone always complained during the rehearsals, but after the show everyone was happy to have participated. After the plays, women and men were invited to participate in a "traditional folk game" in which a woman makes a funny or critical statement about her husband, lover, or boyfriend, who is then asked to respond with a statement about her. Very often jokes were made about female or male partners that made the whole audience laugh. One of my informants told me that it was a game played in villages that gave the women an opportunity to make fun of their partners. Everyone was very relaxed and in a good mood. There was plenty of Vietnamese food for all. Couples with younger children left around 11 P.M., while everyone else stayed for the dance and disco music that lasted until morning. I had agreed with Bui to stay for a while, but finally left after one o'clock.

Since 1965, the student organizations have produced the "European Vietnamese Olympic Games." This "Olympiades des

Vietnamiens en Europe" was created in order to provide greater communication among all Vietnamese organizations under the slogan "sports and friendship." It was also a symbol for the "survival" of Vietnamese culture. The Olympics served to reinforce cultural identity among overseas Vietnamese, particularly the youth. After 1975, the event took on another meaning: political identity. It became the symbol for political unity among refugees. Tran, a leader of a Parisian student association, told me that the competitiveness of the game gives the refugees a sense of collective power. As refugees they tend to consider themselves uprooted and living in a state of dependency. The games reinforce their national pride. Tran believes that such activities increase participation in anticommunist political organizations.

In 1984, the "Olympiades des Vietnamiens en Europe" took place in Marseille from July fourteenth to the twenty-first. I had been invited by Bui, who told me it was the best event of the year. It was the largest social gathering held by European anticommunist Vietnamese organizations, and it was sponsored by the city of Marseille. Participant organizations came from Germany, Belgium, Switzerland, Norway, Denmark, and various cities in France. Each organization was represented by its own team. The team participants (four hundred people) were mostly young male refugees (aged fifteen to thirty-five). Sport activities included soccer, swimming, football, gymnastics, tennis, volleyball, basketball, and ping-pong. The events took place in various recreational areas in Marseille. For a very low fee, participants were given room and board at the dormitory in the Marseille campus of Luminy. It was a hot sunny week in mid-July. The ceremony opened with speeches from the mayor of Marseille and the Minister of the Interior, Gaston Defferre. The event was sponsored by the Association d'Entre-Aide des Vietnamiens d'Aix-Marseille (AEVAM) (Association of Vietnamese Mutual Assistance of Aix-Marseille). AEVAM, renamed in 1975, was formerly the student organization L'Amicale des Anciens Elèves de Saigon (Friendship of Former Students of Saigon), created in 1969. Today the organization's official program is to help Vietnamese refugees integrate into French society. The unofficial goal, as in all Vietnamese anticommunist organizations, is to fight communism in Vietnam.

During the day everyone left the campus to either participate in or watch the sporting events, and in the evening there was entertainment offered by the participants. The blonde Scandinavian girlfriends accompanying their Vietnamese boyfriends led me to believe that these refugees must already speak the languages of the countries in which they were resettled even though Vietnamese was the official language of the event. They formed groups under the flags of the countries they represented rather than mingling together. Teams were very competitive, defending their new country even though they were all Vietnamese. Such behaviors reminded me of school competitions in France and in the United States, where during competition each school team tends to form a supportive homogeneous group. It is also indicative of the process of integration of Vietnamese into their host countries and toward a dual identity, encompassing both the adoptive and the homeland countries, but such a process has not yet been completed since a number of these young Vietnamese had arrived in Europe only a few years earlier.

Another social event that was meant to attract refugees was the Buddha's birthday. In 1984, this celebration took place on a Sunday afternoon in early September. The event was sponsored by the monks of the Khan Anh temple and was held at the Palais de la Mutualité in the fifth arrondissement. There was an entrance fee of twenty francs (four dollars). There were approximately eight hundred people present, mostly refugee families. As was the case at all social events, booths representing social and cultural organizations in the anticommunist networks were set up in the hallways.

Everyone was assembled in the main conference room, and scouts were in charge of helping people find a place to sit. Once again, the South Vietnamese flag in the main room gave a strong political overtone to the religious event. Before the show, a speech in Vietnamese was given by the monk Tro, from Khan Anh. He not only talked about the religious ceremony, but also condemned communism in Vietnam. Then a choir from the Khan Anh temple sang Vietnamese songs, followed by a performance of two traditional Vietnamese dances.

As did the UGVF, the monks of the Khan Anh temple, together with other Vietnamese temples, organized a special social event for the mid-fall children's festival. The event took place in Vincennes, where there was a temple for all Buddhists in Paris. It was a cold, cloudy Saturday afternoon and the event was organized in front of the temple. There was a stage set up for the event, and on one side was a row of chairs where the officials sat with all the monks. There were one thousand refugee parents present along with their younger children. Children between the ages of four and twelve were asked to sit in front of the stage, while their parents stood and watched. No political speeches were given for the occasion. Children were entertained with a children's show and asked to participate in a number of games.

The anticommunist organizations also participated in French-sponsored cultural events. Like the UGVF, they have their own social and political network with French social and political organizations. Bui pointed out that it was important that they participate in social events before a French audience. He explained that they wanted the French people to know that they existed and that the UGVF did not represent the refugee community in France. On a Saturday afternoon in May of 1984, the Foyer International d'Accueil de Paris (FIAP) organized a spring festival, an interethnic event in which Vietnamese, Indians, North Africans, Japanese, Portuguese, Nepalese, and Malagasies were invited to perform. L'Amicale des Vietnamiens de la Région de Paris-Sud and the Association Vietnamienne des Arts, des Lettres et de l'Audiovisuel en France (VALAFRA) (Vietnamese Association of Arts, Letters, and Audiovisual in France) represented the Vietnamese community. Since the audience was mainly French, the entertainment was apolitical, consisting of traditional dances and plays. Nonetheless, in front of the room where the Vietnamese show was presented, all Vietnamese anticommunist political and social organizations had set up their own booths. Everyone else from all the student organizations was there. The event lasted all day.

Leadership and Membership

Like the pro-Hanoi leadership, the anticommunist leadership is primarily composed of educated people. The leaders are former South Vietnamese politicians who wish to regain power in Vietnam. The leaders are either elected by their own political group or self-appointed. Most of the leaders I interviewed were of the older generation and were people who had been members of the Vietnamese Nationalist party that refused to ally with the communists. Tro the pharmacist, for example, said that his brother and father had been killed by the communists. Similarly, Nga, a forty-year-old doctor, told me that although her whole family was anticolonialist, her father had also been killed by the communists.

Members of the various associations are generally educated people. Many are refugees who, though educated, find themselves in a lower class in France than in Vietnam because they cannot get the professional jobs they had possessed in Vietnam. Men and women with the Vietnamese credentials to teach secondary school, for example, now work in French factories or at other manual jobs. Some members are students who want to participate in building the future of Vietnam. Others were formerly students in France who went back to Vietnam after their studies, but then returned to France as refugees after 1975.

Confucian doctrine dictates members' behavior in political organizations. I found that elderly Vietnamese men belong to the leadership organizations, hold authority, and are in charge of decision making in all anticommunist organizations. Younger men and women thus joined the student organizations, although most members of these organizations are educated people in their mid-thirties and no longer students. They cannot become members of the leadership organizations because they are too young. This age-graded hierarchy became very clear to me when I tried to gain access to the leadership organizations through contacts in the student organizations. They told me either that these leadership organizations did not exist or that they did not have the authority to introduce me to any of their members.

The anticommunist groups have great difficulty recruiting members from the larger refugee population. Political leaders claim that many refugees are uneducated people who are more concerned about making a living in France than with the political conflicts of Vietnamese organizations. Van, a forty-five-year-old engineer, said that "most of the young Vietnamese refugees who work in factories are happy to be in France where they can buy cars and material goods and forget about Vietnam." In its appeal to gain support from the Vietnamese refugees, the UGVF has been to a certain extent more successful than the anticommunist organizations. The UGVF cultural events in the community do not carry as many political overtones as the anticommunist ones. The UGVF social programs that help the refugees adapt to France and that are presented to them as nonpolitical organizations have been a major threat to the anticommunist organizations' ability to recruit the refugees and gain their support. But the anticommunist organizations are still successful in their political fund-raising, since most refugees had left Vietnam for political reasons. Over the last few years, however, many refugees have been disillusioned with the political activities of the anticommunist organizations and are reluctant to participate in their activities. Recruitment of new members has thus been predominantly in universities, where students are willing to spend a lot of their time for the cause.

Behind the Bamboo Hedge

In their political discourse, the leaders of anticommunist organizations used the concept of nationalism to mobilize Vietnamese refugees. Like their counterpart UGVF members, anticommunist group members are patriots first, ready to follow political leaders when the well-being of their kin back in Vietnam is threatened. The leaders use the refugees' patriotic sentiments to gain their support against the Vietnamese communists.

Behind the bamboo hedge, leaders admit in private that Vietnamese integration into French society is a fact. Many of them have witnessed the process of integration of the first and second waves of Vietnamese immigrants. Yet, as Bui pointed out, the leaders of political organizations also claim that all refugees will be able to return to Vietnam after the communists are overthrown.

For the refugees, immigration to France was not voluntary, and they persist in claiming that their stay is only temporary. They are preparing themselves for their future role in the inevitable reconstruction of Vietnam. They claim that they are maintaining their cultural heritage to facilitate their eventual return to Vietnam. They worry, for instance, that even temporary adaptation to French society may alienate them even more from their country. As Tuan, a twenty-two-year-old student, pointed out:

Western society offers us a lot of material goods, and we have to make sure that we do not become used to such comfort, because when we return we will have to rebuild a country which cannot offer us all of these goods.

Another Vietnamese informant, Tran, a twenty-eight-year-old businessman, told me that he wanted to move to California, so that he would be closer to Southeast Asia when the communists are defeated. He declared that his business would be oriented toward helping rebuild the Vietnamese economy.

All of these arguments are what I would call political discourse. The reality is that anticommunist leaders are aware of the problems encountered by the long-established immigrants when they attempted to return to Vietnam in 1975. From their point of view, this attempt failed at least in part because the Vietnamese immigrants had become too deeply integrated into French society. As explained in chapters 4 and 5, many of the first- and second-wave immigrants did not return permanently since the social reality of Vietnam did not match their expectations.

Another major concern of the leaders of anticommunist organizations is a weakening of cultural identity among the French-born generation, those raised and educated in French society. It was difficult to detect intergenerational conflict within these organizations in 1984, because most of the French-born generation of refugees were only young children. Despite the French setting, Vietnamese influences remained strong in their upbringing. At an early age, children were taught not only their mother tongue but also the party line. They were expected to side with their parents and continue the struggle to rescue Vietnam from communism.

According to Manh, an anticommunist leader, the home has to be the primary reinforcer of Vietnamese culture and political awareness for the younger generation. Indeed, most Vietnamese refugees do not speak French very well, since in the home Vietnamese is spoken almost exclusively. So far, the Vietnamese refugees have retained their Vietnamese life-style, from food habits to ancestor worship. Vietnamese youths I encountered are also maintaining a certain "Vietnamese life-style" that they do not attribute to any desire to preserve their Vietnamese heritage, but follow simply because they "like it better," as they often told me. Most of them, for example, prefer to eat Vietnamese food rather than French food. Additionally, stories concerning life in Vietnam after the communist takeover, and the family's escape from the regime, are passed down from parent to child. Manh believes that all these elements will contribute to the children's awareness of their responsibilities and duties toward parents and country. He told me that he was spending a great deal of time looking for children who had the charismatic characteristics of potential leaders in the hope that he would eventually be able to train them for the future leadership of these organizations. Many of my leader/informants have similar expectations of their own children. Vo, a seventy-nine-year-old man, said that he would drag his children or grandchildren back to Vietnam if he had to. Many told me that they intended to return with the whole family to help rebuild the country after the communists' defeat.

A few, however, admitted that the rapid integration of Vietnamese refugees and immigrants into French society was making the return to Vietnam less probable. A number of Vietnamese refugees who married French women have children who are no longer Vietnamese and are therefore less likely to return to Vietnam. Nonetheless, others like Lam, a thirty-year-old political activist, demonstrated a continuing commitment to Vietnam by declaring that he would return with his children and leave his French wife behind.

The recruitment of new members is also a current problem for anticommunist organizations, which are mainly focused on Vietnam. In the years following the fall of Saigon in 1975, the refugees were motivated to be involved in anticommunist political organizations. Ten years later, however, the refugees had built new lives in France and were now less interested in political activities. Hai, a leader of L'Amicale des Vietnamiens de la Région Paris-Sud, explained how the organization's membership has dropped over the last few years. In the early years, dedicated student activists spent all their free time working at the organization. Today they are married with children and work at full-time jobs. Hai would have liked to see the coming generation of Vietnamese students taking over the leadership of the student organizations. As he pointed out, most of the leaders of these organizations are former students who are no longer available to spend their weekends and evenings working on political activities. Moreover, young Vietnamese raised in France show less interest in Vietnamese political organizations. Instead, like their French comrades, "they like to dance, frequent bars, and worry about dating," commented Hai. He added that his organization is suffering from a lack of devoted people willing to sacrifice their spare time to organize its many cultural events.

The anticommunist organizations are also competing with the UGVF to solicit members among the working-class Vietnamese refugees who live in the northern suburbs of Paris. The UGVF provides stiff competition by presenting itself to the refugees as a nonpolitical organization and by offering them a number of social services. The defection of working-class refugees frightens anticommunist leaders, who fear their eventual enlistment in labor unions. Ten years after the fall of Saigon, anticommunist leaders can no longer rely on post-flight political fervor to swell their ranks. Like the UGVF did, in order to maintain itself as a political force in the Vietnamese community, the anticommunist organizations will have to shift their political agenda. They will have to address issues of concern to the Parisian Vietnamese community itself, instead of focusing on the refugees' return to Vietnam. In their anticommunist campaign, they will also need to propose more tangible new political goals for possible future social and political changes in Vietnam, instead of focusing on the past and proposing former South Vietnamese leaders for their organization's leadership.

Chapter 7

Conclusion

"To be Vietnamese is to be political." "To lose interest in Vietnamese politics is to lose one's own identity." Such comments are typical of Parisian Vietnamese immigrants and refugees.

This study challenges Cohen's (1969) assumption that political ethnicity is based on the process of "re-tribalization," an idea that suggests that an ethnic group uses aspects of its cultural and social distinctiveness as symbols to mobilize its members and thus compete for political power with other ethnic groups in a highly competitive environment. According to Cohen (1969:190), ethnicity is a political rather than a cultural phenomenon and one that operates, not as an archaic survival device, but within contemporary political contexts. In contrast to other studies on migration, my research shows that Vietnamese immigrants and refugees arrived in their host countries already distinct as a culturally and politically self-identified ethnic group, and their political identity was already embedded in this cultural knowledge, rather than derived from any process of self-assertion as a political interest group. The leaders of overseas Vietnamese political organizations did and still do rely on this common cultural and political knowledge to assert power and authority in their communities.

I define political ethnicity among immigrants and refugees as a process by which a group maintains its cultural and political distinctiveness by promoting homeland political issues within the overseas community. In France, Vietnamese immigrants and refugees have some knowledge and understanding of French politics, but it remains peripheral to what they know about Vietnam. For decades, the Parisian Vietnamese community has exemplified total commitment and devotion to the future of Vietnam.

Vietnamese overseas political organizations played an important role in early anticolonial movements and later in the peace movement to end both American involvement in Vietnam and the war itself. Vietnamese immigrants in France, who had already identified themselves as expatriates hoping to return to Vietnam after hostilities ended, came to realize after 1975 that such a return was not going to be possible. The shift in self-perception from a temporary to a permanent community was especially noticeable in the political agenda of the UGVF, the pro-Hanoi faction. The UGVF has already been establishing itself as a permanent overseas community supporting the Hanoi government. Changes in the organization's political agenda have recently been put forward by French-born Vietnamese, who represent the future leadership of the organization. They are demanding more political autonomy from the Hanoi government and greater emphasis on social and political issues concerning the future of the Vietnamese community in France.

In the French political arena, the Vietnamese community represents a viable political force, yet it is not recognized as an ethnic minority in the sense so common in American political culture. The French Vietnamese, like other Asian ethnic groups, do not constitute a political interest group, since they do not compete for political power within the French political arena. The French government identifies the Asians, along with other nonwhite immigrants, collectively as foreigners, despite the fact that many of them are French citizens.

Racism and ethnocentrism in French society continue to work against the recognition of nonwhite immigrants as ethnic minorities. I use the term *ethnic minorities* here in reference to political interest groups who earn a legitimate right to shape and enact legislation concerning the interests of their own community. The term *ethnic minorities* in France has been commonly used to designate French indigenous ethnic groups such as the Basques, the Bretons, and the Alsacians, among others, whose political activities constitute a threat to French national security (Simon-Barouh 1982).

The new immigrants, especially those from former French colonies like Algeria and other African states, have been treated as second-class citizens and have encountered great resistance in their attempts to be accepted by the French. Simon-Barouh (1982) argues that these immigrants are perpetually labeled as foreigners and so denigrated. When claiming rights in France they are told, "Si tu[1] n'es pas content, retourne dans ton pays; personne ne t'a demandé de venir ici."[2] Thus ignored and rejected by the French people, these immigrants are not politically integrated into French society and remain outsiders despite several generations of residence in France. Unlike Arab and black immigrants, the Vietnamese immigrants have not met with complete rejection by the French. But a "latent" racism among the French toward the new Asian immigrants is likely to emerge with the increasing number of refugees from Southeast Asia as well as the increasing illegal Chinese migration from Asia.

The French Vietnamese thus do not form a politically constituted ethnic minority because there is no political channel in France that would allow them to become an interest group within the spectrum of French politics. As a result Vietnamese immigrants and refugees have had no incentive to identify themselves as an ethnic minority in French society. They have continued to maintain their community as a separate political entity. Although most Vietnamese immigrants and refugees have obtained French citizenship, most of them do not participate in French elections. Instead, they have used their French citizenship mainly for personal reasons like going back to Vietnam or getting a better job in France.

The alliances between Vietnamese political organizations and French political parties provide another example of the ways a separate Vietnamese political identity persists. The two Vietnamese factional political organizations have allied themselves with the French political parties that match their respective ideologies. The UGVF has established its own political network with the French Communist and Socialist parties. In fact, very few members of the UGVF belong to the Vietnamese Communist party, but many of them are members of the French Communist party. The anticommunist organizations offer their community's support

---

1. Note that the use of "tu" with strangers is a mark of disrespect.
2. If you are not happy, go back to where you come from; no one asked you to come here.

to French right-wing political parties in exchange for the Right's support for their own cause. Both Vietnamese factional political organizations have used alliances with the respective French political parties primarily to advance their own political agenda regarding Vietnam.

In the United States many scholars have opted to study immigration in the context of an overall interpretation of the American past, rather than to research immigration and ethnicity in its own right (Archdeacon 1985). For most of the twentieth century, studies about immigrants have relied on the theory of the "melting pot" (Gordon 1964). This theory assumes that newcomers should and would adapt to the mores of the host society. In the late 1960s, the civil rights movement in the United States compelled theorists to recognize that, at least in the case of nonwhite minorities, the melting pot model did not apply. American ethnic groups have responded to prevailing social conditions with ethnic minority politics that challenge the strategies and goals of the melting pot model. Such special interest groups have an established position in the political apparatus of American politics. Ethnic minorities such as the African-Americans, Asian-Americans, and Mexican-Americans have thus attained recognized political power in American society. These newcomers have the option of entering the American political arena as "special interest groups" using the already established political channels available to all American ethnic minorities. The process by which immigrants become an ethnic minority is not, however, assimilative. It instead leads to a dual political identity, one related simultaneously to the homeland and to the host country.

In contrast to the French Vietnamese, the Vietnamese-Americans do have the option of being recognized as an ethnic minority. And yet they do not represent themselves as an ethnic minority. Skinner and Hendricks (1979) argue that an "institutionally defined self-identity" is being imposed on the Indochinese as a precondition for their being considered as an ethnic minority in American society. I argue that, still perceiving themselves as foreigners, the first generation of Vietnamese refugees in America do not yet identify themselves as an American ethnic minority because they have not integrated into their realm of knowledge the concept of minorities, which entails a relationship to a dominant majority culture and the sharing of subordinate status with other ethnic minorities. Vietnamese youths, however, are already identifying themselves as a minority in American society. In my current research in the American Vietnamese community in Oakland, California, I find that this phenomenon is especially noticeable among Vietnamese juvenile delinquents, who perceive themselves as an ethnic group constantly discriminated against by the larger society. Furthermore, the Vietnamese community leaders are able to utilize political channels to benefit the Vietnamese community, as well as to lobby for certain American foreign policies toward Vietnam.

Studying the phenomena of homeland politics enhances our understanding of Vietnamese immigrants and refugees in France and their adaptation to and integration into French society as a group, not just as individuals. I have emphasized the group rather than individuals in an attempt to understand the Vietnamese people from an inside perspective. Dumont (1977) indeed argues that in Eastern societies like China and India, the group is more highly valued than the individual, whereas in Western societies the individual is primary. Influenced by China for a thousand years of domination, Vietnamese society has been modeled according to the Chinese social order, which is primarily based on Confucian doctrine. De Vos (n.d.) suggests that Confucianism socialized people to develop a self that is socially rather than individually oriented. "Behind the bamboo hedge" lies an invisible and powerful Vietnamese community with its own social networks and political organizations. As in the nineteenth-century Vietnamese village, the overseas Vietnamese enclaves have managed to keep foreigners outside the gates of their community life.

This study has focused on factionalism in order to unravel the political conflicts among the various Vietnamese political organizations and to reveal the political intrigues brewing behind the bamboo hedge of the Vietnamese community. The division of the Parisian Vietnamese community into two political factions, pro-Hanoi and anticommunist, is derived from a clash of political ideologies in the history of Vietnam. Factionalism has affected all social institutions in the Vietnamese community: families, for instance, as well as social and religious organizations, both Catholic and Buddhist, have been politically divided along these lines.

Vietnamese political organizations represent the gates of the Parisian Vietnamese community. But since they are factionally divided, they present two different political discourses about the community. The UGVF members, in the pro-Hanoi faction, stress integrating the Vietnamese into French society, maintaining Vietnamese cultural identity, and creating a community to support the Hanoi government. They said that since 1975 they had no longer been involved in political activism, and they dismissed any significant threat from the anticommunist organizations. The anticommunist organizations' members, on the other hand, focus on competing with the UGVF for political power in the Parisian Vietnamese community by trying to gain support among newly arrived refugees and by directing political action against the Hanoi government. They also want the refugees to believe that they will be able to return to Vietnam after an overthrow of the communist Hanoi regime.

I use an analysis of political discourse to understand the nature of Vietnamese political factions. In their respective political discourses, members and leaders of each faction view their community and Vietnam within the context of a political ideology that they see as the "truth." Foucault (1980:131) states that "each society has its regime of truth, its 'general politics' of truth: that is, the types of discourse which it accepts and makes function as true." "Truth" as far as they are concerned is indeed reflected in the political discourses of my informants, who presented their community and Vietnamese politics according to their respective organizations' political lines. This issue of the "political" basis of accepted truth became clear to me from the case of two performers in the Vietnamese Theater who went on a European tour in 1984 and disappeared while in West Germany. My anticommunist informants told me that these two people took the opportunity provided by the tour to defect from Vietnam and seek asylum in West Germany. My UGVF informants, in contrast, told me that these two performers had been kidnapped by Vietnamese anticommunist organizations in West Germany and that anticommunist leaders were using the case for political propaganda against Hanoi. Thus, each Vietnamese political group has its own interpretation of a single fact, and each considers its own version of this event "the truth" and the opposing faction's version a gross distortion of truth.

Behind these two political discourses lie other realities. The Hanoi government needs financial support from the overseas Vietnamese community and is threatened by the Vietnamese anticommunist organizations' political activities. A good example of this hidden agenda is the fact that a number of Vietnamese social organizations sponsored by the UGVF reveal no evidence of their affiliation with the organization, nor is any social event such as the Tet celebration advertised as being sponsored by the UGVF. And whereas the anticommunist organizations' leaders promote the idea that the new refugees will go home after the Vietnamese communist regime is overthrown, they also know full well that most such refugees will settle in France like their predecessors.

Although factionalism has split the Parisian Vietnamese community, it is also a dynamic force that reinforces Vietnamese political identity, which I define as patriotism. Vietnamese patriotism means being faithful to one's country, but does not presuppose loyalty to the political leadership in power (Huynh Kim Khanh 1982). Simmel (1955:11) suggests that "conflict is thus designed to resolve divergent dualism; it is a way of achieving some kind of unity, even if it be through the annihilation of one of the conflicting parties." Patriotism is the main force that keeps the Vietnamese community unified.

Patriotism has been the main force behind Vietnamese resistance movements against such foreign intervention as Chinese domination and French colonialism (Huynh Kim Khanh 1982; Le Thanh Khoi 1955; Woodside 1971). Patriotism has been used by the leaders of Vietnamese political organizations as a mechanism for reinforcing group cohesiveness. Leaders of both the pro-Hanoi and the anticommunist political organizations use culture as a symbol to articulate political alignments within the community in order to gain the support of Vietnamese immigrants and refugees. In their political discourse, the leaders of the respective political organizations invoke patriotism to legitimate and promote their own political and nationalistic programs. The UGVF leaders claim that Vietnam under communism is an independent country, whereas leaders of anticommunist Vietnamese organizations claim that Vietnam is not an independent country at all, but is indirectly controlled by the Soviet Union.

Factionalism among Vietnamese immigrants and refugees

will persist as long as there are Vietnamese political organizations whose political agendas focus exclusively on Vietnam. Throughout history, political activism and factionalism have characterized the Parisian Vietnamese community, and they are likely to continue regardless of what political party is in power in Vietnam.

Behind the Bamboo Hedge also challenges our own representation of non-Western immigrants and refugees in industrial societies. Studies on migration have focused essentially on economic integration, social adaptation, and the extent to which a group is able to maintain its own culture in the new environment. Immigrants and refugees are thus expected to melt into full membership in the host society, on the assumption that their homeland political ties have no relevance to their emergence as an ethnic group in their new country. This study on homeland political activities enhances our understanding of the process that keeps such migrant groups in overseas communities from being any more than partially integrated into the host country because it reveals how adamantly they wish to maintain their dual political identity.

While the recognition of a dual cultural identity among immigrants and refugees has been largely studied in social sciences, very little has been written about the process of a dual political identity. The concept of a dual political identity implies the socioeconomic integration of an immigrant community into the host country, along with the simultaneous development of the overseas community's political allegiance to both the homeland and the host country. The Vietnamese immigrants and refugees in France and in the United States present a very good case study of the development of this dual political identity. In the first stage of adaptation into French and American society, homeland politics is the central feature in Vietnamese political organizations. As the immigrants and refugees begin to realize that they will not return to Vietnam and are permanently settled in France or in the United States, they become increasingly concerned with American and French domestic political issues regarding their community. Nonetheless they are entering respective political arenas of the French and American societies as a politically well-organized community, represented by their respective political organizations. In order to maintain their leadership in the community, these Vietnamese political organizations have to address in their political agenda issues concerning both Vietnam and their own overseas community.

Comparative studies on political activism among other immigrant and refugee groups such as the Palestinians, Armenians, and Afghans should further our knowledge of how these groups are integrating into the host country with a dual political identity and of the extent to which these international overseas political networks have an impact on homeland politics.

Bibliography

Albertini, R. Von
1971   *Decolonization: The Administration and Future of the Colonies 1919–1960.* New York: Doubleday and Co.

Archdeacon, T. J.
1985   Problems and Possibilities in the Study of American Immigration and Ethnic History. *International Migration Review* 19:112–32.

Archives Nationales de France, Section Outre-Mer
1929– Paris: Service de Liaison avec les Originaires des Territoires de la France
37   Outre-Mer.

Aron, R.
1968   *L'Opium des Intellectuels.* Paris: Gallimard.

Banerian, J., ed.
1985   *Losers Are Pirates: A Close Look at the PBS Series "Vietnam: A Television History."* Phoenix, Ariz.: Sphinx Publishing.

Barth, F.
1969   *Ethnic Groups and Boundaries.* Boston: Little, Brown and Co.

Benedict, B.
1957   Factionalism in Mauritian Villages. *British Journal of Sociology* 8:328–42.

Boissevain, J.
1966   Patronage in Sicily. *Man* 1(1): 18–33.

Bonvin, F., and F. Pinchaud
1981   *Insertion Sociale des Réfugiés du Sud-Est Asiatique.* Paris: Recherche Sociale. No. 78 (April–June).

Boudarel, G., ed.
1983   *La Bureaucratie au Vietnam.* Vietnam-Asie-Débat-1 Série. Paris: L'Harmattan.

Brisset, C.
1984   *Le Monde,* November 9.

Brocheux, P., and D. Hemery
1980   Le Vietnam Exsangue: Echec Economique, mais Détermination Politique. *Le Monde Diplomatique*, March.

Bujra, J. M.
1973   The Dynamics of Political Action: A New Look at Factionalism. *American Anthropologist* 75(1): 132–52.
Buttinger, J.
1972   *A Dragon Defiant: A Short History of Vietnam*, 2 vols. New York: Praeger Publishers.
Carkroff, R. P.
1979   *New Economic and Social Opportunities for Americans and Vietnamese on the Texas Gulf Coast.* Washington, D.C.: Trans Century Corp.
Chesneaux, J.
1955   *Contribution à l'Histoire de la Nation Vietnamienne.* Paris: Editions Sociales.
Cohen, A.
1969   *Custom and Politics in Urban Africa: A Study of Hausa Migrants in Yoruba Towns.* Berkeley and Los Angeles: University of California Press.
1974   *Two-Dimensional Man: An Essay on the Anthropology of Power and Symbolism in Complex Society.* Berkeley and Los Angeles: University of California Press.
Condominas, G., and R. Pottier
1982   *Les Réfugiés Originaires de l'Asie du Sud-Est.* Paris: La Documentation Française.
DeLey, M.
1983   French Immigration Policy since May 1981. *International Migration Review* 17:196–211.
Devillers, P.
1952   *Histoire du Viêt-Nam de 1940 à 1952.* Paris: Editions du Seuil.
De Vos, G.
1976   Introduction: Change as a Social Science Problem. In *Responses to Change: Society, Culture and Personality*, edited by G. De Vos. New York: Van Nostrand Co.
n.d.   Confucian Family Socialization: The Religion, Morality and Aesthetics of Propriety. In *Self Society and Minority Status*.
Dictionnaire Larousse
1971   Paris: Librairie Larousse.
Direr, F.
1982   La Coopération Franco-Vietnamienne. *Association d'Amitié Franco-Vietnamienne, Bulletin d'information et de Documentation*, No. 42/43 (January–February:14–17.
Doan Van Toai with D. Chanoff
1986   *The Vietnamese Gulag.* New York: Simon and Schuster.
Dumont, L.
1977   *From Mandeville to Marx: The Genesis and Triumph of Economic Ideology.* Chicago: University of Chicago Press.
Duncanson, D. J.
1968   *Government and Revolution in Vietnam.* London: Oxford University Press.

Durkheim, E.
1912 *Les Formes Elémentaires de la Vie Religieuse: Le Système Totémique en Australie.* Paris: Librairie Félix Alcan.

Fall, B.
1963 *The Two Vietnams: A Political and Military Analysis.* New York: Praeger Publishers.

Fitzgerald, F.
1973 *Fire in the Lake: The Vietnamese and the Americans in Vietnam.* New York: Vintage Books.

Foucault, M.
1980 *Power/Knowledge: Selected Interviews and Other Writings 1972–1977.* Edited by C. Gordon. New York: Pantheon Books.

Gallissot, R.
1984 L'Interrogation Continue: Minorités et Immigration. In *La France Au Pluriel?* Paris: CRISPA, Revue Pluriel-Débat, Editions l'Harmattan.

Gauthier, J.
1949 *L'Indochine du Travail dans la Paix Française.* Paris: Editions Eyrolles.

Gibson, J. W.
1988 *The Perfect War: The War We Couldn't Lose and How We Did.* New York: Vintage Books.

Girardet, E.
1980 *Christian Science Monitor*, November 25.

Girardet, R.
1972 *L'Idée Coloniale en France: 1871–1962.* Paris: Editions la Table Ronde.

Gordon, M. M.
1964 *Assimilation in American Life: The Role of Race, Religion and National Origins.* New York: Oxford University Press.

Gough, K.
1978 *Ten Times More Beautiful: The Rebuilding of Vietnam.* New York: Monthly Review Press.

Gourou, P.
1936 *Les Paysans du Delta Tonkinois: Etudes de Géographie Humaine.* Paris: Les Editions d'Art et d'Histoire.

Hemery, D.
1975 Du Patriotisme au Marxisme: L'Immigration Vietnamienne en France de 1926 à 1930. *Le Mouvement Social,* No. 90 (January–March): 3–54.

Hickey, G. C.
1964 *Village in Vietnam.* New Haven: Yale University Press.

Hoang Van Chi
1964 *From Colonialism to Communism: A Case History of North Vietnam.* New York: Frederick A. Praeger.

Ho Chi Minh
1967 *On Revolution: Selected Writings, 1920–1966.* Edited by B. Fall. New York: Praeger.

Huard, P., and M. Durand
1954   *Connaissance du Viêt-Nam*. Hanoï: Ecole Française d'Extrême-Orient.
Huynh Kim Khanh
1982   *Vietnamese Communism 1925–1945*. Ithaca, N.Y.: Cornell University Press.
Kahin, G. McT.
1987   *Intervention: How America Became Involved in Vietnam*. New York: Anchor Books.
Kelly, G.
1977   *From Vietnam to America: A Chronicle of the Vietnamese Immigration to the United States*. Boulder, Colo.: Westview Press.
Kennedy-Brenner, C.
1979   *Foreign Workers and Immigration Policy: The Case of France*. Paris: OECD Development Center.
Kunz, E. F.
1973   The Refugee in Flight: Kinetic Models and Forms of Displacement. *International Migration Review* 7:125–46.
Lacouture, J.
1968   *Ho Chi Minh: A Political Biography*. Translated by P. Wiles. New York: Vintage Books.
Lamb, H. B.
1972   *Vietnam's Will to Live: Resistance to Foreign Aggression from Early Times through the Nineteenth Century*. New York: Monthly Review Press.
Lasswell, H.
1931   Factions. In *Encyclopedia of the Social Sciences*, vol. 5. New York: Macmillan.
Leach, E. R.
1954   *Political Systems of Highland Burma*. London: G. Bell.
Le Huu Khoa
1983   *Les Vietnamiens en France: La Dialectique de l'Insertion-Identité*. Ph.D. diss., University of Nice.
Le Thanh Khoi
1955   *Le Vietnam: Histoire et Civilisation*. Paris: Editions de Minuit.
1978   *Socialisme et Développement au Viêt-Nam*. Paris: Presses Universitaires de France.
Liu, W.
1979   *Transition to Nowhere: Vietnamese Refugees in America*. Nashville: Charter House Publishers.
McAlister J. T.
1969   *Vietnam: The Origins of Revolution*. New York: Alfred A. Knopf.
McAlister, J. T., ed.
1973   *Southeast Asia: The Politics of National Integration*. New York: Random House.
McAlister, J. T., and P. Mus
1970   *The Vietnamese and Their Revolution*. New York: Harper and Row Publishers.

Magagnini, S.
1985 *San Francisco Chronicle*, October 7.

Mangalam, J. J., with C. Morgan
1968 *Human Migration: A Guide to Migration Literature in English, 1955–1962*. Lexington: University of Kentucky Press.

Marcilly, J.
1984 *Le Pen sans Bandeau*. Paris: Jacques Grancher, Publisher.

Marr, D.
1971 *Vietnam Anticolonialism, 1885–1925*. Berkeley and Los Angeles: University of California Press.
1981 *Vietnam Tradition on Trial: 1920–1945*. Berkeley and Los Angeles: University of California Press.

Mignot, M.
1984 *Les Réfugiés du Cambodge, du Laos, du Vietnam en France: Un Centre d'Hébergement, une Commune, une Région d'Accueil et d'Insertion*. Vienna: W. Braumuller.

Montero, D.
1979 *Vietnamese Americans: Patterns of Resettlement and Socioeconomic Adaptation and Assimilation in the United States*. Boulder, Colo.: Westview Press.

Nguyen Khac Vien
1983 Les Spécialistes du Discours Politique Creux aux Postes Clefs et l'Inflation Bureaucratique. Translated by Bui Xuan Quang. In *La Bureaucratie au Vietnam*, edited by G. Boudarel. Vietnam-Asie-Débat-1 Série. Paris: L'Harmattan.
1974 *Tradition and Revolution in Vietnam*. Berkeley: Indochina Resource Center.

Nguyen, S. D.
1982 Psychiatric and Psychosomatic Problems of the Southeast Asian Refugees. *Psychiatric Journal of the University of Ottawa* 7:163–72.

Nicassio, P. M.
1985 The Psycholosocial Adjustment of the Southeast Asian Refugee: An Overview of Empirical Findings and Theoretical Models. *Journal of Cross-Cultural Psychology* 16:153–73.

Nicholas, R.
1965 Factions: A Comparative Analysis. In *Political Systems and the Distribution of Power*, edited by M. Banton. A.S.A. Monograph 2. London: Tavistock.

Nicolson, H.
1934 *Peacemaking, 1919*. London: Constable & Co.

Noirel, G.
1984 L'Histoire de l'Immigration en France, Note sur un Enjeu. *Actes de la Recherche en Sciences Sociales* 54:72–76.

Osborne, M. E.
1969 *The French Presence in Cochinchina and Cambodia: Rule and Response (1859–1905)*. Ithaca, N.Y.: Cornell University Press.

Patti, A. L. A.
1982   *Why Vietnam? Prelude to America's Albatross.* Berkeley and Los Angeles: University of California Press.

Phan Thi Dac
1966   *Situation de la Personne au Viêt-Nam.* Paris: Editions du Centre National de la Recherche Scientifique.

Pike, D. E.
1969   *War, Peace, and the Viet Cong.* Cambridge: M.I.T. Press.

Plender, R.
1972   *International Migration Law.* Leiden: A.W. Sijthoff.

Popkin, S. L.
1979   *The Rational Peasant: The Political Economy of Rural Society in Vietnam.* Berkeley and Los Angeles: University of California Press.

Portes, A., and R. L. Bach
1985   *Latin Journey: Cuban and Mexican Immigrants in the United States.* Berkeley and Los Angeles: University of California Press.

Portes, A., and R. Mozo
1985   The Political Adaptation Process of Cubans and Other Ethnic Minorities in the United States: A Preliminary Analysis. *International Migration Review* 19:35-63.

Rath, J.
1983   Political Participation of Ethnic Minorities in the Netherlands. *International Migration Review* 17:445-65.

Redfield, R., R. Linton, and M. J. Herskovits
1953   Memorandum for the Study of Acculturation. *American Anthropologist* 38:149-52.

Roberts, S. H.
1929   *The History of French Colonial Policy: 1870-1925.* London: P.S. King and Son.

Siegel, B. J., and A. Beals
1960   Pervasive Factionalism. *American Anthropologist* 62:394-417.

Simmel, G.
1955   *Conflict and the Web of Group-Associations.* Translated by R. Bendix. London: Free Press of Glencoe.

Simon, P. J.
1981   *Rapatriés d'Indochine: Un Village Franco-Indochinois en Bourbonnais.* Paris: Editions l'Harmattan.

Simon-Barouh, I.
1982   Minorités en France: Populations Originaires des Pays de l'Asie du Sud-Est. *Pluriel Débat*, No 32:59-70.

Skinner, K. A., and G. L. Hendricks
1979   The Shaping of Ethnic Self-Identity among Indochinese Refugees. *Journal of Ethnic Studies* 7:25-41.

Starr, P. D., and A. E. Roberts
1982 Community Structure and Vietnamese Refugee Adaptation: The Significance of Context. *International Migration Review* 16:557–94.

Stein, B. N.
1979 Occupational Adjustment of Refugees: The Vietnamese in the United States. *International Migration Review* 13:25–45.

Strand, P.
1984 Employment Predictors among Indochinese Refugees. *International Migration Review* 18:50–59.

Strand, P. J., and W. Jones, Jr., eds.
1985 *Indochinese Refugees in America.* Durham, N.C.: Duke University Press.

Sullivan, M. P.
1978 *France's Vietnam Policy: A Study in French-American Relations.* Westport, Conn.: Greenwood Press.

Swartz, M., ed.
1969 *Local-Level Politics: Social and Cultural Perspectives.* Chicago: Aldine Publishing Co.

Swartz, M., V. Turner, and A. Tuden, eds.
1966 *Political Anthropology.* Chicago: Aldine Publishing Co.

Thuan Cao Huy
1984 Les Réfugiés du Sud-Est Asiatique en France et aux Etats-Unis. In *La France au Pluriel?* Paris: CRISPA, Revue Pluriel-Débat, Editions l'Harmattan:139–60.

Tran Tam Tinh
1978 *Dieu et César: Les Catholiques dans l'Histoire du Vietnam.* Paris: SUDEST-ASIE.

Truong Nhu Tang with D. Chanoff and Doan Van Toai
1986 *A Viet Cong Memoir: An Inside Account of the Vietnam War and Its Aftermath.* New York: Vintage Books.

Viet Tran
1979 *Vietnam: J'ai Choisi l'Exil.* Paris: Editions du Seuil.

Wilson, A.
1983 *Refugees Newsletter*, No. 24 (December): 11.

Wong, B.
1982 *Chinatown: Economic Adaptation and Ethnic Identity of the Chinese.* New York: Holt, Rinehart and Winston.

Woodside, A.
1971 *Vietnam and the Chinese Model: A Comparative Study of Nguyen and Ch'ing Civil Government in the First Half of the Nineteenth Century.* Cambridge: Harvard University Press.

1976 *Community and Revolution in Modern Vietnam.* Boston: Houghton Mifflin Co.

Yacono, X.
1973 *Histoire de la Colonisation Française.* Paris: Presses Universitaires de France.

Index

AEVAM, Association d'Entre-Aide des Vietnamiens d'Aix-Marseille (Association of Vietnamese Mutual Assistance of Aix-Marseille), 161

Afghan leader: at Vietnamese demonstration, 153, 154

Algerian youths, 124

Alliance Vietnamese, L' (The Vietnamese Alliance), 63, 141

American: intervention, 36; Vietnam War, 37; offensive, 53; withdrawal, 40, 69; interventionist policy, 53

American ethnic groups: African-Americans, 172; Armenian-Americans, 1; Asian-Americans, 172; Chicanos, 77; Cuban-Americans, 1, 78; Japanese, 77; Jews, 77; Mexican-Americans, 172. *See also* Ethnic groups; Ethnic minorities

Amicale des Anciens Elèves de Saigon, L' (Friendship of Former Students of Saigon), 161

Amicale des Vietnamiens de la Région de Paris-Sud, L' (The Friendship Association of the Vietnamese of South Paris), 64, 140, 141; leadership of, 140; membership of, 167; as representative of Vietnamese community, 163; Tet celebration of, 159, 160

Amitié Franco-Vietnamienne (Franco-Vietnamese Friendship Association), 126. *See also* UGVF

Ancestral: cult, 95, 120; altar, 95; anniversary, 96

Anticolonial movements (also activities): overseas, 31, 32, 33, 35, 170; in Paris, 47, 56, 60, 66, 81; in Vietnam, 28, 31, 38

Anticommunist associations, underground, 64. *See also* Freedom fighters

Anticommunist faction, 22, 32, 33, 36, 37, 38, 39, 41; core of, 64; leaders of, 156. *See also* Anticommunist organizations

Anticommunist organizations (Vietnamese), 39, 46, 53, 54, 59, 60, 63, 64, 67, 70, 77, 85, 87, 93, 96, 97, 105, 145, 146, 148, 149, 150, 151; and campaign against UGVF, 153; and competition for power, 152; and competition with UGVF, 168, 174; and effort to rebuild the country, 167; European, 161; French-born generation, 166; intellectuals of, 143; leaders of, 153–54, 158; leadership of, 90, 141, 143, 156, 163, 166, 168; network of, 142, 162; political and social network of, with French political and social activities, 152; and political discourse, 152, 165; and